THE ACTION HERO TEACHER 2

Teachers of the Lost Class

Karl C. Pupé FRSA

COPYRIGHT

© 2022 Copyright actionheroteacher.com

All Rights Reserved.

This book or any portion thereof may not be reproduced or used in any manner whatsoever without the express written permission of the publisher, except for the use of brief quotations in a book review.

Printed in the United Kingdom

First Printing, 2022

ISBN

For more details, visit the author's website at www.actionheroteacher.com

DEDICATION

This book is dedicated to all the 'lost kids'.

The kids who grew up without anyone in their corner to tell them that they believed in them.

The kids who grew up 'on the wrong side of the tracks'.

The kids that grew up in households of abuse, drug-addiction, neglect and despair, without anyone to come and rescue them.

The kids who were picked on because they were different.

If you were one of these kids, then pat yourself on the back. You're still here and clearly you're trying to make your life better. This will make you even more valuable to the students you teach.

Never give up on yourself – the world needs your dreams, wisdom and skills more than ever.

I salute you.

PRAISE FOR KARL C. PUPÉ AND *THE ACTION HERO TEACHER: CLASSROOM MANAGEMENT MADE SIMPLE*

Karl's approach to relationships and behaviour is fresh, credible and burns with authenticity. His work is practical and instantly usable. I wouldn't hesitate to recommend him.

Paul Dix, educator, behaviour specialist and best-selling author of "When The Adults Change"

This is an inspiring and practical read… I devoured it — the style is open, funny, compelling and accessible. For teachers, it's a brilliant hands-on guide to dealing with difficult situations… Don't let teachers hog this amazing book! I would give it six stars if I could.

Viv Groskop, best-selling author of "How To Own The Room", stand-up comedian, TV and Radio Presenter

Karl has delivered several webinars for the NEU on classroom management. His expertise is deep and wide-ranging, but his real gift lies in how he communicates his subject. He is warm and funny and his pop culture references are impeccable! He is a treat to watch and to engage with. Highly recommended.

Jacqui O'Neill, National Professional Development Manager for the National Education Union (NEU)

Karl is a confident speaker with a modern style of delivery, making him very engaging to listen to and easy to relate with. His approach consisted of sound theoretical knowledge accompanied by great practical examples that explained the presented concepts clearly to our early career teachers. Karl has a true passion for what he does and his experience really shines through in his presentation. A pleasure to work with and one of the best presentations I have seen in my time working at the Chartered College of Teaching.

Paul Williamson, Networks and Events Manager, Chartered College of Teaching

This really is a great read, showing you a different perspective on how to manage young people with difficult behaviour in a teaching environment. It really has become my aide-memoire in the classroom... brilliant book!

Michelle Myrie, Grants and Learning Officer at Youth Music

Karl is a passionate educational leader... His open and honest approach in what he writes is also his presentation style. He speaks from the heart and eases the audience into a safe space through his authentic presence... He is a visible role model in his ability to be authentic, straight-talking and positive in sharing constructive solutions to systemic problems.

Hannah Wilson, Leadership Development Consultant and Founder of #DiverseEducators

Very insightful! Karl is bursting with information and passion toward supporting Generation Z students. You'll come away from his session with new skills and considerations.

Katie Caplehorn, Outreach Team, University of Essex

He is a thought leader and huge inspiration in the field. His charisma, work ethic and commitment to the cause of social justice reveals him as a consummate professional. He is definitely one to watch and his name will firmly be rooted in folklore of education innovation.

Kevin "KJ" Brazant, Learning Development Specialist and founder of Lounge Akademics Studio and Daddy's CPR

Karl is a powerful and passionate speaker who truly knows how to engage an audience... He is highly recommended.

Ethan Bernard, Co-founder of the award-winning 'Aspiring Heads' programme

Having first come across Karl's work during lockdown, I have been following his writing and presentations ever since. I have read and listened to *The Action Hero Teacher* more times than I care to admit. It is a staple of my CPD programme, both personally and at school, particularly around behaviour. I've also had the pleasure of speaking with Karl on my podcast, and his classroom-rooted, motivational and actionable advice speaks to teachers directly. I highly recommend Karl's work and cannot wait to read more.

Phil Naylor, author of 'Naylor's Matter' and creator of the 'Naylor's Natter' Podcast

TABLE OF CONTENTS

Copyright ii
Dedication iii
Praise for Karl C. Pupé and The Action Hero Teacher: Classroom
Management Made Simple iv
A Special Message from Viv Groskop ix

INTRODUCTION 1

Before We Start, Here's a Little Bit About Me and The Action Hero
Teacher 2
So, Why Write a Sequel? 7
Who Is This Book For And How Is It Different From AHT1? 10
How to Use This Book 13
Eight Signs you are in a Toxic School and Why you Need to
Leave Pronto 18

TEACHING GENERATION Z 26

Teaching Generation Z 27

THE BASICS 38

Trust Mountain – a Refresher 39
The Flashpoint Triangle 44

ESCALATION 52

Escalation Introduction 53
Young People and Mental Health Part 1: The Facts and the Theories 54
Young People and Mental Health Part 2: Relationships are the Key
to Dealing with SEMH Students and Here's Why 64
Learn to be 'Rude': Use Pattern Interrupts to Take Control of
Tricky Conversations 75
Make 'em Scared to Lose: Learn How to Use Negativity in a
Positive Way 87

vii

DISENGAGEMENT/HOSTILITY 98

Disengagement/Hostility Introduction.. 99
The Leadership Zone Part 1 - The Persona and the Shadow: Why You Must Get to Know the Real You 100
The Leadership Zone Part 2: How to Build Your Leadership Persona 107
The Leadership Zone Part 3: What Jürgen Klopp Can Teach you About Classroom Leadership – A Case Study.. 120
Meet 'The Disruptors' – The Six Types of Characters That Will Ruin Your Lessons and How To Deal With Them 133

AUDIENCE 152

Audience Introduction 153
Group Dynamics 101: If You Don't Control the Crowd, the Crowd Will Control You 154
Argue Like a Pro: How to Have Meaningful Conversations in the Age of Social Media Without Kicking Off... 165
Help Them Make Better Decisions 180
Be a Giver: How to Use 'The Law of Reciprocity' to Enhance Your Classroom Relationships 194

EPILOGUE 202

Thank You Ms Pearce 203
Contact Page... 207
Acknowledgements 208
Bibliography... 209

A SPECIAL MESSAGE FROM VIV GROSKOP

What is that thing they say about teaching? "Those who can… do. Those who can't… teach." What a miserable and misrepresentative way to talk about the toughest job in the world. It's probably one of the most famous quotes on teaching in history, taken from George Bernard Shaw's 1905 play Man and Superman. And yet it's a complete misunderstanding of teaching and the value we should place on it. Teaching is not secondary to other activities. Nor it is a substitute for doing other things. Teaching comes first and is the cornerstone and foundation of all our lives. Many of us owe everything that we are and everything that we believe about ourselves to great teaching. Many of us form closer relationships with teachers than we form with members of our family. In some cases, teachers are even likely to give us information more reliable and more sensible than the information passed on to us by our own families.

Even though we may not all teach during our lifetime, every single one of us will be taught by someone. We deserve teachers who are happy and fulfilled in their work, supported, appreciated and well-rewarded. In my own experience of being taught both as a child and an adult, the best teachers are the ones who could have done anything in life but chose (and chose is the operative word as teaching is truly a vocation) to teach. If you have chosen to teach, then we are lucky to have you. And if teaching is your calling, then you won't find a better place for support, advice, comfort and comradeship than you will alongside Karl Pupé. As well as being experienced, compelling and inspiring, he is also pretty funny. And, like all the best teachers, he's just as likely to laugh at himself as he is at anyone or anything else. When it comes to this book, that makes his own teachings really easy and fun to read. Again, just like all the best teachers, you won't feel like you're being taught.

I first met Karl in 2019 when I was speaking at a teaching conference about presentation and performance. My own background is in broadcast journalism and stand-up comedy. My experience comes from podcasting, radio and television and being on stage on the stand-up circuit, from hosting tours for people like Graham Norton and Dawn French and from slogging away with one-woman shows at the Edinburgh Fringe. Most people think of these things as being daunting, like the scariest version of public speaking. We all know the Jerry Seinfeld quip about funerals: we'd rather be in the coffin than giving the eulogy, right? But I know first-hand that these situations are often far less intimidating than facing a class of students. When I was in my early twenties, I taught occasionally — mainly as a TEFL teacher (Teaching English as a Foreign Language). I'm also close to my sister who has been a secondary school teacher for twenty five years. So, I'm acutely aware of the challenges, rewards and pitfalls of teaching.

My role at this conference on the day when I met Karl, though, was a simple one: to pinpoint the complementary skills that exist in the worlds of education and entertainment. What do comedians have to teach educators about holding an audience's attention? And what could performers learn from teachers about humility, authority, resilience and parking your ego at the door?

On this particular day, I really wanted it to be a practical workshop, full of advice and the sharing of stories, rather than a dry, theoretical discussion. So I asked the participants to form into groups and report back on various questions. Karl led a group and when he fed the group's ideas back to the room, he instantly struck me as someone who knows how to play a crowd, when to be sensitive and how to summarise difficult information.

He talked about his own experiences with alienated students, especially those excluded from the mainstream education system, in a way that was discreet and respectful but also open and authentic. And he talked about how you win people round when they really don't want to listen to you. I was completely blown away by his energy and his determination. The point I was trying to make that day about teaching being similar to stand-up comedy — only more difficult — was perfectly made.

I've had many conversations with teachers over the years about the similarities between the classroom and the stage. You need to write your own material and keep it fresh. You need to win them round in the first thirty seconds. You can get heckled at any moment. And you're up there on your own with no-one to help you. (So much so that you might often regret not having chosen to be part of a double act...) Compared to comedy, teaching will always be the harder job. Your "audience" comes to know you over time so you can't repeat your material. You need to form a personal relationship with everyone who comes into your orbit. And you need to adjust your material so that it speaks to each person in the room. A stand-up needs to transform a group of individuals into a crowd. A teacher has a much tougher gig: they need to speak to a group whilst also speaking to every individual in that group. Even harder to achieve, those individuals have to take something away from that encounter and apply it elsewhere, whether in life or in an exam room or both. On stage you just need to connect in the moment. In the classroom you need to create a connection that is going to have an effect in later life. A stand-up can say words that are forgettable and disposable. A teacher must speak in a way that is memorable and lasting.

The major difference between comedy and teaching is that your students have often not chosen to be in school. They are forced to go. In comedy, your audience are adults and they have paid for a ticket. So in some ways in comedy if they don't like you, it's their fault not yours. They chose the wrong comedian. They can choose another show next time or they can switch TV channels. In teaching, your task is much harder: you have to make yourself "liked" without seeming to want to be "liked." No teacher is allowed to say: "Too bad, you chose the wrong teacher." You must make yourself into the right teacher for every class because your class can't switch channels. That requires the courage, stamina, mindset and self-belief that Karl's exercises will breathe into you. When I read his first book, *The Action Hero Teacher*, I understood more about Karl's message: that with the right insight, flexibility and listening skills, you can become a better teacher. With *The Action Hero Teacher 2*, he broadens these ideas and introduces more inspiring stories and examples which will encourage you to bring a flavour of this bravery and creativity into your own life and teaching.

We need teachers who can make a mockery of that awful George Bernard Shaw quote and transform it into what it should read: "Those who choose to teach... deserve our eternal gratitude because it's bloody difficult." Or maybe: "Those who can... teach. Those who don't... are wimps." It might take a while for my one-woman mission to bear fruit as I spread that message. So, in the meantime sit down with *The Action Hero Teacher 2* and take as many notes as you can. You will never feel less alone. Instead you will feel braver, bolder and considerably better-equipped to face whatever teaching — or the world — throws at you.

Viv Groskop is a comedian and author of *How to Own the Room*, **also a chart-topping podcast.**

Listen to our episode from March 2020 for an interview with Karl Pupé: https://howtoowntheroom.libsyn.com/natalie-and-karl-pup-teachers

INTRODUCTION

BEFORE WE START, HERE'S A LITTLE BIT ABOUT ME AND THE ACTION HERO TEACHER

Don't Call This a Comeback.

- LL COOL J

Hello treacles. I'm going to go out on a limb and bet that you've read my first book, *The Action Hero Teacher: Classroom Management Made Simple*. But if you haven't, allow me to re-introduce myself. My name is Karl C. Pupé FRSA and I've been knocking around education for over a decade.

Some of my roles have included:

- A trained teaching assistant, providing one-to-one support to children with severe Special Educational Needs (SEN) and Social, Emotional and Mental Health needs (SEMH).
- A fully-qualified teacher.
- NEETs Coordinator, specialising in teaching vulnerable 15-19-year-old students to mitigate anti-social behaviour and bleak life-outcomes.
- A youth mentor.
- Doing supply teaching in Inner City London (successfully).
- As the Alternative Provision Lead in a mainstream school, I was in charge of devising an alternative curriculum

designed to retain and engage students at risk of permanent exclusion.
- Earning an ILM Level 4 Certificate in Leadership and Management.

So, now we have the CV stuff out of the way, let's talk a little bit more about *The Action Hero Teacher* and why you are holding this lovely tapestry of folksy wisdom in your hands. In early 2017, I left Alternative Provision, thanks to the Government's austerity cuts and found myself in the hustle-and-bustle of mainstream education.

Coming from a background of dealing with learners who like to swear first and ask questions later, and sometimes throw the occasional chair at my head, I thought teaching mainstream would be... easy.

How wrong I was.

For me, behaviour management in mainstream settings was even WORSE than Alternative Provision. In my mainstream colleagues, I found a group of dedicated, professional, yet exhausted educators who had too many things to do, yet so little time to do them.

Additionally, they were tired of doing the same ole CPD, telling them to do the same ole things without a result. My colleagues, often surprised that I didn't get eviscerated by the various 'characters' that stalked the school like xenomorphs, would approach and ask me for help to engage these troubled young souls.

My abilities weren't because I was special, but through the machinations of fate, I ended up in many teaching and non-teaching roles that helped me deal with difficult people. My story is all in my first book – I did some jobs that you won't even believe…

So, like a tipsy co-worker mustering up the courage to talk to their year-long crush at the office Christmas party, I put my observations, thoughts and strategies into a wee book that became *The Action Hero Teacher*.

I never had a book deal or a budget for marketing and promotion. My social media presence consisted of my Facebook page showing embarrassing images of my university raving days. I've taken them down a while ago. I know how you think – nosey parker.

I released my book extremely quietly on Friday 8th March 2019, making a short WhatsApp video in front of my skinny, red bookshelf in my Super Mario pyjama top. Clearly, I didn't know what I was doing, but my uncle texted 'Well-done mate', so that's all that counts.

I think I sold 30 copies of *The Action Hero Teacher* in the first year. They were mostly to my friends, relatives and a kind supply teacher that I managed to coerce into buying the book. My book-writing superstardom failed to launch, and I didn't get to drink a pina colada in the five-bedroom Portuguese villa I'd built up in my vivid imagination. I resigned myself to doing lunch duties in my bright orange hi-viz vest, eating a soggy custard crumble while pleading with the kids not to kill each other in the playground.

But in Year 2, things started to pick up momentum. In the torture that was lockdown, I started a blog at actionheroteacher.com to help more educators and give away free resources. Word-of-mouth began to spread. Like Boris Johnson 'accidentally' being at his birthday party during the restrictions, things started to change rapidly in ways I couldn't imagine.

At this time of writing, almost four years on, here's a brief list of what AHT (and I) achieved.

- Actionheroteacher.com was voted one of the 'Top 10 Most Influential Education Blogs' in the UK by vuelio.com, a prominent marketing and software company.
- Learning Ladders, in association with Twinkl.com, awarded the AHT book one of the 'Top 40 Best Books for Educators Summer 2021'.
- I managed to facilitate workshops for prestigious education organisations, including the National Education Union, Charted College of Teaching, University of Essex, Youth Music, Teach First and the National Education Group.
- I was inducted into the Practitioners Council for the Foundation of Education, an independent advisory board to UK policymakers to promote better education practices and frameworks for all UK students.
- And in September 2021, I was awarded a fellowship in the prestigious Royal Society of Arts, Manufacture and Commerce (The RSA) for my AHT workshops promoting the well-being of young people. (My family were so proud – this London boy did good.)

For the record, I'm eternally grateful to all the people that helped to make AHT the success that it is. I know it sounds like I'm bragging, but I mean it.

This is also why I love Super Mario. Forget you, Sonic.

SO, WHY WRITE A SEQUEL?

Good question. Writing a book is tricky, and I'm not rich enough to hire a fancy ghost writer.

After I wrote my first book in 2019, I quietly went back to using Microsoft Word to write school reports and send complaint letters to my local borough about the lateness of their rubbish collectors – true story.

Then 2020 happened.

Brexit finally kicked in. The COVID-19 pandemic. Global lockdowns. George Floyd's murder. Black Lives Matter. Escalating climate change disasters. The 2020 US Election unleashed an insurrection. The political divide became a canyon. Russia invades Ukraine. The horrors of wars, catastrophes and terror are streamed through social media in real-time 4K HD.

Our world became like a Jerry Bruckheimer film that none of us wanted to be in and, Bruce Willis couldn't 'yippee-ki-yay' us out of trouble.

The global madness continues at this time of writing and we are STILL not entirely out of the woods with COVID. We have lived through a collective trauma and our kids bore the brunt of it.

Like many of you, I've become used to watching the news through my fingers, and I just want to click my heels like Dorothy in *The Wizard of Oz* and make it all go away. But it is not about us, is it?

I've spoken to students so disenchanted with our political, social and educational systems that they think it's all a waste of time.

After witnessing the soaring university costs and shrinking job opportunities (especially for those from underprivileged backgrounds), I've spoken to students who think that learning is a 'sucker's game' that serves the elite few.

I've spoken to students who get thrown by the wayside because of their complex needs and they know it. Unfortunately, these students become the victims of a tick-box culture that sees them as a set of statistics on a league table rather than unique individuals.

I've spoken to teachers who have gone part-time to do a full-time job because of the enormous workload. I've spoken to support staff who do an absolutely heroic job dealing with the complex needs of their students, against the backdrop of reduced funding and lack of help in these chaotic times.

I've seen our profession get bashed all over the press and the media, especially during COVID, despite many of us risking our well-being to give first-class care to the students who desperately needed it.

And we wonder why our kids are 'playing up' more in school? People, this isn't just poor behaviour – it's trauma.

INTRODUCTION

I could go on and on, but if you have picked up this book, I will bet on my favourite Avengers socks that you are acutely aware of our challenges.

I hope this second book builds on my first one, helping you shepherd your young charges through these desperately disruptive times, and making you look damn good while doing it.

Despite what the papers, the media and our society say, you are valued because you literally change lives every single day.

I salute you and hope this book will help you become a behaviour management kung-fu master.

But first, let me explain who this book is for.

WHO IS THIS BOOK FOR AND HOW IS IT DIFFERENT FROM AHT1?

Good question. Like the first book, this text is for:

- Trainee teachers and support staff.
- Educators who have a class full of 'goblins' they need to tame quickly.
- Educators with excellent subject knowledge, but can't quite crack how to build relationships with their students.
- Educators who teach SEMH students that want a couple more tricks in their toolbox.

But this is where AHT2 ups the ante: I have two simple aims:

1) To educate you about Generation Z (and Generation Alpha). These two groups are the first human generations of the Information Age and are like no generation that has ever come before. They are the first generations to never know what life was like before the Internet, and now they have an IMAX cinema seat to one of the most pivotal times in human history. Using research and a bit of common sense, my job is to give you a bird's eye view of how these revolutionary times shaped our students' worldviews and attitudes. Then, armed with this knowledge, you will get an 'edge' on how to teach and engage these 'digital natives'.

2) Take a deep dive into the mind of your 'disruptive students'. This book aims to drill deeper into the psyche of 'Disruptors' – these are the students who make your classes unteachable, making you pull out those beautiful locks of your strawberry-scented hair. This book aims to 'get under the skin' of our more disruptive learners and look at ways you can build better relationships and protect your boundaries while we push them higher up 'Trust Mountain'. (If you read AHT1, you will know what this is; if you haven't, there's a refresher coming in the next section.) Combined with the techniques in AHT1, this will make you a formidable classroom teacher.

We will look at psychology, social anthropology, mental health practices, sales, marketing, sports, and even rap music to help us get these kids onside.

But... let me tell you what I won't do.

My job is NOT to make you into a mental health professional or a psychologist. Let me use the following analogy to explain what I mean.

The Paramedic and The Surgeon

If you have watched any realistic hospital TV dramas, you will have seen what a paramedic does. For example, suppose you come across a person who is severely injured and is non-responsive, lying on the ground. You call the ambulance services to assist. Very soon, a paramedic will arrive at the scene of an accident, assess the victim and provide life-sustaining treatment to take them to the hospital.

But have you ever seen a paramedic do an operation on the roadside? Or have you ever seen them set up a tent to provide week-long care off a major motorway? This wouldn't happen because they don't have the tools nor the means to ensure the person receives the best care. Their job is to stabilise the patient and signpost them to the correct people (aka the emergency doctors) who will be able to carry out deeper assessments to make sure they get what they need.

Likewise, as educators, we are not psychologists – we do not diagnose our students regarding their mental health or give our 'treatment plans' to try to 'fix them'.

There are some SEMH students whose needs are extremely complicated and delicate. Unfortunately, it is not within our gift to help them, and sometimes our uninformed attempts may make their challenges worse. Always remember, your aim is:

a) To create a stable, safe, affirming environment with clear boundaries that will mitigate their triggers or help them come out of their 'fight-or-flight' states.

b) To signpost young people to the correct individuals or departments who can help them address their needs.

The word 'paramedic' can be broken into two words. 'Para' means 'alongside', and 'medic' means 'doctor'. Paramedics work with the doctors but don't attempt to do their jobs.

You are an educational paramedic – you don't do the nitty-gritty, emotional work of a mental health professional, but work as part of a team to help our children to thrive.

OK. Now we have covered that, in our next section, let's look at how to make this book work for you.

HOW TO USE THIS BOOK

Okily dokily, neighbour.

It's time to reintroduce you to the 'Action Hero Teacher Original Recipe' for behaviour management, but in the AHT tradition, let me hit you with the disclaimers.

1) This is NOT a Storybook

As much as I amuse myself (and hopefully you), this book isn't designed to be read like the latest John Grisham novel. Instead, this book is split into sections, focusing on a specific part of behaviour management. The goal is to work through those sections and hone your 'particular set of special skills' like Liam Neeson.

In a typical chapter, I will say something funny, introduce you to a theory, look at its practical uses in the classroom and get you to reflect. The chapters are meaty, but I want to give you that sweet value you crave.

By all means, please have a skim read of the book from cover to cover. But I want it to be a reference book you can dip in and out of as you please. I know that you have 1,000 books to mark, a Head of Department that is on your back and a personal life to enjoy, so if you read ten pages of AHT2 and it helps you, my job is done – although I hope you paid for this book… I have kids to feed.

2) You Will Have to Put in the Work

Look, I want a body worthy of *Love Island*; trust me, I've tried every fad diet to locate my six-pack that disappeared 18 years ago. But I know that without steroids, it won't come back overnight. So likewise, although these tips and tricks are designed to be easy to implement in your classrooms, you'll have to practice them to become second nature.

At the end of each chapter will be a series of reflection questions to help you mull over what you have learned, and practical tips that will help you embed them into your practice. Please, please, please get a little notepad and write down the answers. Or, at the very least, think about what is being asked. You will never improve in anything in life if you don't reflect on what you are doing. Sometimes, all it takes is a little tweak to give you the breakthrough you desire, which is my aim with these checkpoints. If you don't do the work, this book will tickle your ears, but Johnny Tableflipper will still be flipping tables at you with impunity. That's not good for your health.

3) This Text Builds Upon My First Book, *The Action Hero Teacher*

I say this unashamedly. Although I have added some new theories and tips for you, I will be referencing a little bit of the stuff I wrote in AHT1. In addition, where appropriate, I will give you brief summaries of the theories and strategies I established in my debut text. Finally, to keep the book relatively short, I may just either refer you to a chapter in the old book or put a link to a blog post on actionheroteacher.com. They'll usually be at the end of the chapter in tiny writing.

Don't worry. This book will still help you, and you don't have to buy the old book (although it would be nice). Think of AHT1 as the beginner's guide and this book as the intermediate level. If there are any gaps in your knowledge or you are new to behaviour management in general, take a gander at AHT1. Of course, if you have any queries, head to my site – actionheroteacher.com – and drop me a message. I respond very promptly.

4) Adapt it to the Level that You Teach

Like my first book, these principles were designed to be used across all age ranges. Although this book is a more 'advanced' version of my first one, I reckon that 70-80% of what I write here could again be used across all age groups.

Albeit I have worked across the majority of key stages (primary, secondary and further education), I have written this book with slightly older students in mind (Year 7 upwards). BUT, for our early years and primary educators, there is enough stuff in here that would be worth a tenner of money and a couple of hours of your time.

Kids learn how to lie by the time they are two years old (shocking but true), so they are a lot smarter than you think. Scale back the language and 'differentiate' to their appropriate level. Early years and primary school teachers are absolute geniuses at breaking complex concepts down in ways their little bubbas will understand. This will be a piece of cake for you.

5) The Advice in This Book is Not Magical – it's Common Sense

I am not Doctor Strange or Harry Potter. The only magic wand I wave around is the one that turns my TV on and off. So, although I am eternally grateful for the great reviews of my first book, I am aware that I do not have the Eye of Agamotto and what I say is pretty simple.

If you read this text and say, 'Karl, I already do this!' then congratulations, keep on going – but I hope you will have a lot more 'wow-that's-a-really-cool-idea' moments as you read through my musings. I will try to give you the information straight with no chaser. Don't confuse simplicity with ease. As my great uncle once said, 'Common sense is not common practice.'

So, here's the recipe:

Step 1: Read Section 2 (Teaching Generation Z) and Section 3 (The Basics). These sections are mandatory. Section 2 will look at how the macro changes in society affect your students, and Section 3 will give you the theories that underpin the rest of this book. If you don't read them, I will send some heavies to your house.

Step 2: Sections 4, 5, and 6 deal with different aspects of the 'Flashpoint Triangle' (don't worry – you'll learn about it in a bit), which contain practical strategies to help you handle your classes. Have a quick read and highlight any particular tips or tricks you want to try.

Step 3: Once you have reached the book's end, select one strategy from Sections 4, 5 and 6 that you would like to try with your classes. Read the Reflection Questions, answer them (preferably on paper), and look at the practical tips for guidance on how to implement them.

Step 4: Once you have reflected, try them out. Do this for at least a week and then reflect on what went RIGHT or what went WRONG. If it worked, congratulations, you're the bee's knees! If it didn't work, that's OK too; try another tip that may suit your style better. Once you have mastered the techniques you like, go back to step 2, rinse and repeat.

The aim is to help you achieve mastery, and we can only do that by deliberate practice. Don't worry – if you follow this recipe, you will master 'The Force' in no time. So, let's keep moving, young Skywalker.

But, my dear colleague, I must give you a warning. None of this stuff will work if you teach in a 'toxic school'. In the next chapter, you will find out why.

EIGHT SIGNS YOU ARE IN A TOXIC SCHOOL AND WHY YOU NEED TO LEAVE PRONTO

You Are Not Batman

In the dead of the night, you stand on the lonely rooftop, watching the hapless criminals dragging the ATM machine out of the battered door, twitching and hurried. The rain patters on your tactical assault suit, pleading for you to stop, but you shrug it off, ready to ambush your prey.

In the blink of an eye, you pounce. Your punches crunch on the terrified thugs' faces. Confusion. Fear. Screaming then blackness. The criminals have been caught, the money has been secured, and you, Batman (Batwoman or Batperson), have saved the day. You call the Commissioner to pick up these miscreants and slink off your base to rest.

But the next day, on the same roof at the same time while on patrol, you see the same criminals doing the same thing that you caught them for yesterday.

What the actual bleep, bleep, bleep is going on here? (I'm going to keep it professional.)

This would probably make for a great comic book movie, but if I were Batman, I would be ticked right off, fella.

INTRODUCTION

How do the Dark Knight's tribulations relate to us humble educators? A lot more than you think.

For some of you, this is your typical school day. You have a disruptive student who makes your life hell. You deal with the disruptive student. You sanction them/call home/plead/cry/sing lullabies/call the King's Guard, but STILL, nothing happens. You listen to people like me and attend all the CPDs in the world to help you, but Johnny Tableflipper is still flipping tables and flipping you 'the bird'.

So, you start to question yourself and ask, 'Am I a bad teacher?' This is not what you signed up for. That Sunday night dread evolves into Sunday night depression at the thought of having to face 'that' class on Monday, Period 2.

What in Boris Johnson's name is happening here?

Behaviour does not occur in a vacuum. You could be the best behaviour manager in the world, but if your school does not support your efforts, you are doomed to be like Batman, standing on that roof, punching the same criminals in the face for eternity. That's not fun.

Eight Signs your School has a Toxic Behaviour Culture

In recent years, there has been a growing conversation about working in 'toxic schools'. There are many reasons why a school can be toxic and some explanations can be pretty complex.

No school is perfect, nor do I expect them to be. The vast majority of teachers only want what is best for their students, and they work damned hard to give the best quality education that taxpayers can buy.

Since writing AHT, I have been fortunate to talk to many educators around the country about their toxic experiences. Unfortunately, I have noticed familiar patterns that keep coming up in our dialogues. Do a mental checklist and see if these themes keep occurring in your organisation.

1. Denial of Poor Behaviour

If I see a small bird that likes lakes, has green and grey feathers and often makes a quacking sound, for the love of all things sweet and tasty, I'm not going to call it Kendrick Lamar.

But unfortunately, some organisations would insist 'what you are saying is wrong', and of course, the little ducky is the multi-Grammy award-winning rapper and entrepreneur and 'you need to get your eyes checked'.

In all seriousness, if your school looks like something out of *The Purge* and you are being regularly insulted, assaulted or ridiculed by your students, but leadership still deny the behaviour is bad, that's a red flag.

If those responsible for behaviour downplay or even gaslight you into thinking that being told to 'eff off' is acceptable because 'we are a _____ school in _____ area', you need to start backing away slowly.

2. The Behaviour Policy is Confusing

Some organisations' behaviour policies are overly complicated and contradictory. These policies have a million rules and so many subclauses, you would think you are trying to solve a geopolitical crisis using the UN Charter.

If you ask a reasonable student to name the basic rules of the school and the kid makes a perplexed face like he is trying to let off a difficult fart, it doesn't bode well for you. If the students have trouble understanding what they are required to do, then guess what? They won't know the boundaries and will play up in your class. Happy days.

3. Communication is Poor

Different schools have different ways of managing behaviour – that's granted. But one of the key ingredients to a thriving school environment is open communication.

If you passed an issue to a Head of Year, would they get back to you in a reasonable time? If you have been assaulted or had a nasty lesson, would the pastoral team or senior leaders check if you are OK?

Of course, there are a million ways that you can do this – take your pick. But if you are constantly stonewalled or communication feels like you are a character trapped in Christopher Nolan's *Tenet* movie, then that's a very, very bad sign.

4. Some Students are Persistently 'Let Off' Sanctions

Imagine you follow everything to the letter. You have warned the student, followed the protocol and given the sanction, believing the matter has been resolved. If you discover that the young person was 'let off' by someone higher up the chain and you are never informed why, something smells of rotten tuna sandwiches here.

Sometimes, there are mitigating circumstances and things in the background that you are unaware of. But, if this repeatedly happens with the same students but there is never any explanation, this could pose serious problems for you down the line. In some schools I've heard of, some students escape punishment better than Mafia Dons – this is not good.

5. Your Feelings are Easily Dismissed

Tragically, this tends to happen more with Early Career Teachers. For example, imagine you have just started in your school and have been on the receiving end of abuse. You raise your concern to your Line Manager and they dismiss it, saying 'that's just part of the job' or 'you need to toughen up'. This puts you in an awkward position where you feel you must minimise the bad things happening to you.

That is not OK.

Our job is difficult. You can't fake being a good teacher. Our non-teaching friends could probably go on a bender the night before and stagger into their cubicle incognito. As long as they sound and act the part, they can skate through their day A-OK.

Teachers can't do that.

When you stand in front of your classroom with 30 pairs of eyes clocking your every move, there is nowhere to hide.

If you stubbed your toe and you had an epic meltdown, I understand why your boss might feel you need to 'straighten yourself out'. But if you raise legitimate concerns that are constantly undermined, this is toxic to your well-being. So please don't ignore this.

6. Toxic Leaders

This goes without saying. Run for the hills if you have leaders who behave like James Bond villains and treat you with utter contempt. Toxic behaviours from the top tend to leak to the bottom until the whole organisation is rotten.

If you want to play 'Toxic Leader Bingo', look out for the following traits:

- Lack of empathy
- Pathological lying
- Arrogance
- Never listens to feedback
- Passive aggressive to a fault
- Lazy/incompetent (or both)
- Throws everyone under the bus (Machiavellianism)
- Dictatorial
- Sensitive and petty
- Constantly must remind people that they are the 'Boss'

If your boss is a Homelander wannabe – it's time to bounce.

7. A Hostile Environment

I understand that teaching's not a walk in the park. Tempers get frayed, and your patience can be whittled down to a stub. But if every time your colleagues or seniors stare in your direction, you feel strips of skin flying off your back – this is very toxic.

Overt aggression is horrible, but passive aggression is too. If you work in an environment where people give back-handed compliments, undermine you, sabotage your work, suck all the joy out of the room and like to gossip about you, this will be devastating to your mental health.

Why is this relevant to behaviour management? Because our young people are not stupid. They pick up on these vibes, and some of the more vindictive students may use this negative energy to their advantage, such as pitting two or more teachers against each other. Yes – this can happen. I have seen it with my own eyes.

8. Inaccessible Leadership

Again, 99% of our school leaders do an impeccable job under immense pressure. Especially over the last two years, with so much volatility in the world, they have led us bravely, effectively and tirelessly – sadly, often with a high personal cost to themselves.

They're not who I am talking about.

If you have a behaviour issue that you try to present to management but trying to find them resembles an episode of *Where in the World is Carmen Sandiego?*, you're in for a rough time. Leaders who do not respond to your communications in a reasonable time (or ever) also count.

Leaders, and any teaching professionals for that matter, should give professional courtesy to respond to issues promptly or at least signpost you to someone that can help. Complete silence is not fair and makes your job ten times harder.

No school is perfect because no humans are perfect. I expect the best schools in the land to have one or two of these traits. But if you're reading this and saying: "OMG Karl, do you follow me to work? This is exactly my school!" Then OMG, get the heck out.

Seriously, six or more traits suggest a very, very toxic school, and over time, this will erode your mental, emotional and even physical health. Unfortunately, no training will change this type of environment – I'm sorry, this book won't help you.

In the immortal words of comedian Jim Carrey, "Before you diagnose yourself with depression or low self-esteem, first make sure you are not, in fact, just surrounded by a$@holes.[1]"

I tell you this: you won't be able to help anyone if you are in a state. So, don't let a toxic school push you into poor health. It's not worth it.

Now we've got all that out of the way, let's talk about 'Generation Z' (and Alpha) and what makes them so unique. Hang on to your butts.

TEACHING GENERATION Z

TEACHING GENERATION Z

First Things First... What the Heck is a Generation?

The *Cambridge Dictionary*[1] defines a generation as: "All the people of about the same age within a society." A new generation occurs every 12-20 years. If you teach learners born between 1997-2012 (8-25 years of age), they are Generation Z. Children born after 2012 are now classified as 'Generation Alpha' or 'Generation C', as they were raised during the COVID-19 pandemic.

Why does this matter?

We are all shaped by the generations that we emerge from. Our beliefs, language, ideas and worldviews are moulded in the times that we inhabit. Your worldview determines how you interact with reality.

Harvard psychologist and one of the pioneers of modern psychology, William James in 1890 wrote, "In most of us, by the age of thirty, the character has set like plaster, and will never soften again[2]."

So what happens to your brain as it ages?

From the time you are born until your mid-twenties, your brain's neural network is incredibly elastic and fluid. When you are younger, your brain's flexibility makes it easier to:

1) Be more creative.
2) Learn and absorb new information quicker.
3) Be willing to adopt new ideas and worldviews.

But after the age of 25, your neural network starts to 'set', and we tend to become 'stuck in our ways'. Sadly, many of us become less flexible in our thinking, leaning more toward our experiences than our imaginations. That's why it's said, "It's hard to teach an old dog new tricks."

Dr Tara Swart, a neuroscientist and leadership expert states, "Our brains are inherently lazy and will always choose the most energy-efficient path[3]."

This also explains why we have generational conflicts. But again, because of our brain's biology, as we age, we are literally not on the same wavelengths of thought as the previous or later generations. And this causes friction.

As newer generations emerge, their different views challenge the previous generations' paradigms, leading to misunderstandings, stereotypes and insults.

I'm sure you have heard some of these classics...

- Okay Boomer
- Millennials are entitled/lazy
- Gen X'ers are psychos

You get the point.

But as author and strategist Robert Greene in his book *The Laws of Human Nature* states, "Knowing the characteristics of each generation allows you to break free from their constraints[4]." So today, you will gain what Greene called 'generational awareness' to tap into the Gen-Z students.

The most well-known model is called the 'Strauss-Howe Generational Theory'. This was established by authors and historians William Strauss and Neil Howe in their 1991 book *Generations*, which they continued to expand upon. Their initial studies focused on American History, but they did the same research on other civilisations and saw similar trends.

According to their theory[5], human history tends to repeat itself over 80-100 years, which they called a "saeculum" (pronounced see-que-lum).

A saeculum goes through four distinct phases called "turnings", and each new generation that emerges has its own political, economic and cultural ideas that differ from the generation before.

Each new generation develops a 'persona' that typifies the group's behaviours and norms.

According to their theory, the four distinct phases are High, Awakening, Unravelling and Crisis. The first turning, known as the 'High' turning, usually comes after a period of great upheaval and a new stable societal order emerges. Trust and compliance with civic and public institutions are at their highest, and individualism is frowned upon. In this era, the public consciousness is focused on the collective and the greater good.

But as the years roll on and further generations emerge, questions about the new order appear, and apathy and distrust amongst the populace start to take shape. Individualism and social splits begin to occur, with more people calling for a change in the culture. Finally, at its lowest point, during the 'Crisis' turning, a significant threat emerges, which galvanises the populace to confront it. This crisis is the catalyst to finally tear down the old system and replace it with a new one, repeating the cycle.

Of course, every generation faces crises, but how they respond to them determines their characteristics. In the fourth turning, the crisis generation proactively tries to establish a new status quo, leading them into direct conflict with all the other generations who want to reform but not dismantle the system.

Of course, in recent history, The Great Depression of 1929 could be seen as the start of the great crisis in the 20th Century. This prompted the rise of far-right extremism, two world wars, and a complete re-ordering of the world order as Nazi Germany was defeated. That generation was known as the 'Golden Generation', who were at the forefront of these profound political, economic and social changes that we still use today.

This sentiment was also echoed by American investor and philanthropist Ray Dalio in his book, *Principles for Dealing with The Changing World Order*. Like the Strauss-Howes' model, he used the term 'Big Cycles' to identify the 100-year shifts in human history and the rise and fall of world powers.

He wrote: "These periods of destruction/reconstruction devastated the weak, made clear who the powerful were and established revolutionary new approaches to doing things (i.e. new orders) that set the stage for periods of prosperity... that produced new stress tests and deconstruction/reconstruction periods[6]."

Of course, no one theory is perfect – we have to apply nuance – but they are good guidelines to help us understand the cultural shifts in our world. With our ever-deepening environmental crisis, polarised politics, the COVID-19 pandemic, tense race relations, and our public institutions' inadequate responses to these issues, mean that we teach a crisis generation.

Here are a few facts that we've gathered about the latest generation coming through the ranks.

1) Generation Z Are Entrepreneurial

Gen Z and Alpha carry something daily that Sir Isaac Newton, Leonardo Da Vinci, Galileo and Albert Einstein could only dream of.

What is it?

A smartphone.

The phone in your pocket has more processing power than the computers that put Man on the Moon.

Generation Z are' Digital Natives' – the first human generation to never know what life was like before the Internet.

With the Internet democratising ownership, fame and influence, our students no longer feel that they must go through the cultural and societal 'gatekeepers' to get their projects and ideas into the world. Instead, they have a powerful 'do-it-yourself' attitude.

Creativity, side-hustles and entrepreneurship are the new rock 'n' roll.

As well as listening to musicians and following actors and sports stars, this generation is just as comfortable consuming content from social media influencers and Internet entrepreneurs like KSI, Gary Vee, Maya Jama, Chunkz and Yung Filly, Logan Paul and PewDiePie.

In a KPMG study about Millennial/Gen Z work patterns, researchers found[7]:

- 65% of Gen Z'ers stated they expect to leave their current jobs within 2 years.
- 75% were considering joining the 'Gig Economy' – temporary, flexible jobs where employers hire independent contractors instead of salaried staff.
- On average, Gen Z workers stayed in a job for 3 years and felt comfortable "looking for new challenges".

Reasons cited for their ease of movement were:

- Online networking opportunities
- Peer-to-peer comparisons of other companies are more accessible than ever, which helped them make faster decisions.
- Low entry barriers to create independent streams of income outside conventional employment. Online marketplaces like Amazon and eBay and cheap website-building platforms like Wix and Squarespace make it incredibly easy for young people to start online stores and trade internationally.

Your students are ambitious and may challenge your authority because they may see the old way of doing things as 'obsolete'.

There are also strong indications that this generation has grown disillusioned with our current education system as they feel it inadequately prepares them for the real world.

2) Generation Z are Pessimistic about Authority

According to a 2019 Deloitte study, when interviewing older Gen Z'ers, a mere 12% believed that the political and economic situation would change for the better over the next 12 months[8].

For older Generation Z students, many of their defining moments were in the wake of the 2008 Great Recession, government cutbacks, the fallout of the Brexit vote and the chaotic political split it caused. Based on what they have seen over the last decade in these turbulent times, they find it challenging to see any positive outcomes.

Although these students are more uncertain about society's future, they are more entrepreneurial, willing to broaden their horizons, and less frivolous than generations before.

In a survey of 13-39 year-olds by youth marketing website 'YPulse', 72% believed that 'hashtag activism' had the power to change the world, especially in light of the #BlackLivesMatter movement[9].

3) Generation Z are Driven as much by Values as they are by Material Goods

In the last five years, 'cancelling' a celebrity has become an everyday activity on social media.

Celebrities and public figures who have done particularly bad or shame-worthy things, past or present, get 'dragged' (publicly shamed, ridiculed and harassed online).

This is not a new practice according to our human nature. For example, in medieval times, we punished wrongdoers by putting them in stocks or publicly executing them!

But social media has given all of us the power to publicly assassinate another person's character from the comfort of our own homes.

The desire to seek justice and correct past wrongs is a key feature of a crisis generation. According to market research group Ipsos Mori[10], less than 30% of students felt that the things they owned said much about their socio-economic status, compared to 42% in 2011.

The report revealed, "Despite (the) pressure of a harder economic context, there has been a cohort shift away from materialistic values."

In the UK, Generation Z was raised during the 2008 Great Recession and government austerity measures that followed. They also recognise the stark wealth inequality gap between the richest and poorest members of society. As a result, these students are more sensitive to issues around equality and fairness and more willing to express their views across different mediums.

But let's not forget that Generation Z are no longer the new kids on the block. Remember, kids born after 2012 are known as Generation Alpha. So, although these little teenie-boppers can barely get onto funfair rides, they are starting to make their presence felt. And we've got a little data on them too.

Here are five facts about Generation Alpha:

1) By 2024, 2 billion humans on the planet will be classified as 'Generation Alpha'. This will make them the largest generation in the history of the world[11].

2) Research indicates that 36% of 8-11-year-olds, after school, spend most of their time speaking to their friends online, compared to 28% who would see them in person[12].

3) On average, Generation Alpha uses 4.2 streaming services (this includes YouTube), with 59% of Gen Alpha stating 'streaming movies' is their most popular activity outside gaming, social media and music.

4) More time online means they are less likely to be supervised, with 68% of 8-11-year-olds using devices and consoles without direct parental supervision.

5) Social media platforms have flourished post lockdown, with TikTok outpacing the Meta suite (Facebook, WhatsApp, Instagram), with an 18% increase in 2022 alone[13].

Back in my day, my idea of entertainment was a large box and a really, really good imagination. These guys have access to technology that would make our grandparents think that the Starship Enterprise existed. Our youngsters stand on the cliff edge of history, and we must guide them.

OK folks, let's take a little breather. I have given you a shedload of information. Answer the questions below.

REFLECTION QUESTIONS

1. Think of a class that you teach. Or, if you don't teach, think of a group of young people you interact with regularly. Do you feel they're different from how you were at their age? What do they do differently? What are the positives and negatives of their modern attitudes?

2. What is your impression of how technology influences young people? Do you think it has a positive or negative effect? Has technology changed the way that you interact with your young people?

3. Do you feel young people are not as respectful to authority as they were in the past? Think about a time recently when you witnessed a flashpoint situation with a young person. How was it handled? Would it have been handled differently if this had happened during your childhood/adolescent years?

Recognising your own biases when dealing with your young people is vital. For the reasons I explained above, although they seem like aliens to you, hopefully this chapter will give you a new lens to view them through and offer a different way to interact with them.

So, now I have given you the lowdown on Generation Z, the rest of the book will look at strategies to engage them.

Let's move on to the basics.

THE BASICS

TRUST MOUNTAIN – A REFRESHER

When it comes to classroom management, I developed a mental model that has served me very well over the years, called 'Trust Mountain'. I first wrote about this in AHT1. If you already know the theory and don't need the refresh, please skip to the 'Flashpoint Triangle' chapter. But for the uninitiated, here's a quick summary.

Trust Mountain was greatly inspired by the acclaimed psychologist Abraham Maslow and his famous "Hierarchy of Needs".

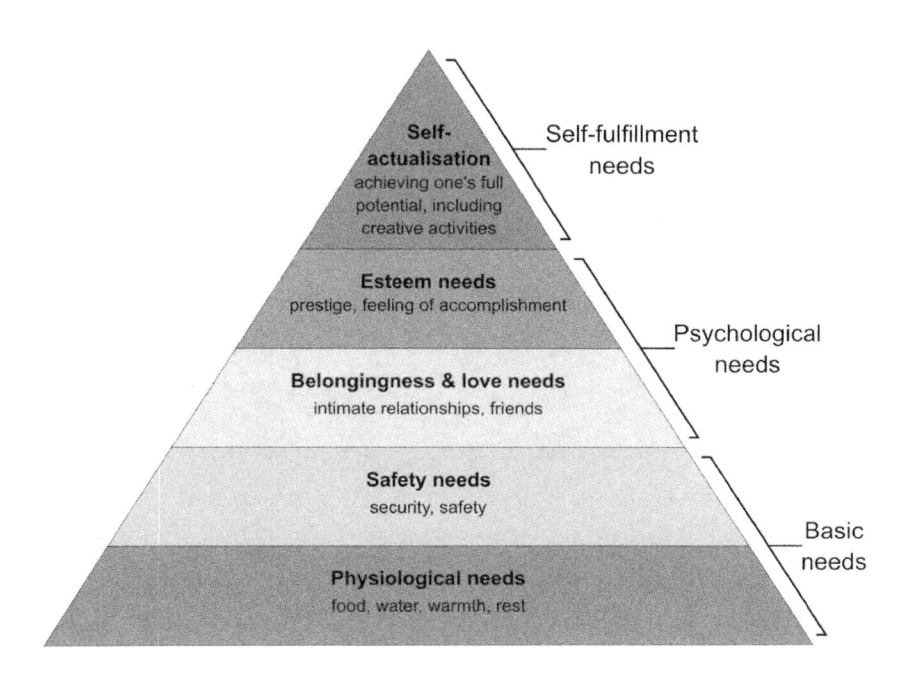

Self-actualisation
achieving one's full potential, including creative activities
— Self-fulfillment needs

Esteem needs
prestige, feeling of accomplishment

Belongingness & love needs
intimate relationships, friends
— Psychological needs

Safety needs
security, safety

Physiological needs
food, water, warmth, rest
— Basic needs

Maslow's Hierarchy of Needs[1]

According to Maslow's theory, if you didn't satisfy the basic needs such as physical safety and shelter, you couldn't advance to the higher stages like purpose and relationships. If I was in a locked room with one million pounds on the table but on the other side of it was a 7ft serial killer that was just about to wake up, I wouldn't be thinking about buying a Bugatti. Once we get rid of the butcher, then we can make it 'rain in the club'.

Likewise, Trust Mountain is quite simple:

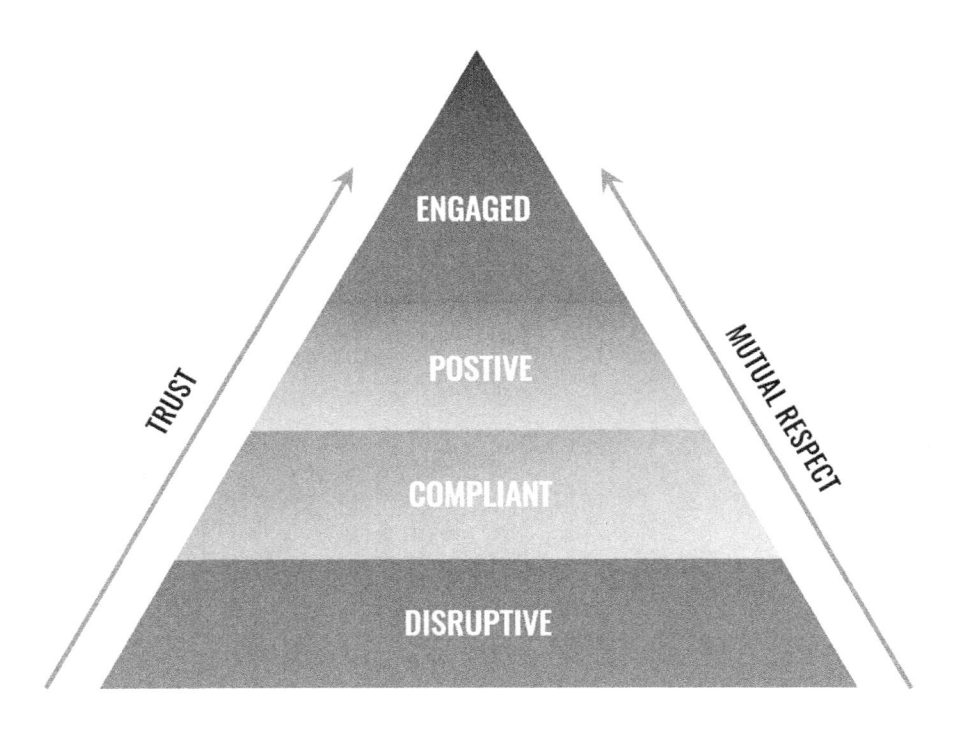

Trust Mountain pyramid, from top to bottom: ENGAGED, POSTIVE, COMPLIANT, DISRUPTIVE. Left side labelled TRUST, right side labelled MUTUAL RESPECT.

The more your students respect you and the more you can build a healthy working relationship with them, the more they will enjoy their lessons and behave positively.

This is demonstrated by having two things:

1. **Authority** - This is where your students respect you as their teacher and respond well to your instructions and guidance.
2. **Warmth** - This is the ability to empathise with your students and understand their needs.

Like Maslow's Hierarchy, our aim is to take our students as high up the mountain as possible. So, let's do a quick tour of the mountain and look at the essential characteristics we can expect from each stage.

1) Disruptive

- The Red Zone.
- Non-existent relationships between the student and the teacher.
- Rules and boundaries are regularly crossed or simply don't exist.
- There are regular firefights and flashpoint situations, i.e. physical fights and verbal abuse.
- No learning takes place.
- It's a hostile environment for everyone.

This is the worst possible outcome and the most stressful. A class full of Disruptors will make you quit your teaching career pronto. Let's keep going.

2) Compliant

- The Yellow Zone.
- Students will follow the rules, but you will have to repeat them several times.
- Home of 'low-level disruption' and the 'classroom jokers'.
- Students at this level have to be micromanaged to stay on task.
- These students tend to push the envelope on what they can and can't get away with.

This level is slightly better as they will listen to you and follow your instructions, but to a minimum level. This is draining but better than chairs being thrown at you.

3) Positive

- The Green Zone.
- The relationship between the teacher and student is positive, and there is mutual respect.
- Students can focus on tasks without fuss.
- Students at this level can 'self-correct' – they will change their negative behaviour with minimal input from you.
- Students want positive reinforcement.

4) Engaged

- The Blue Zone.
- The Dream – this is the stuff you see on the 'Get Into Teaching' adverts.

- Students fully engage in your lessons, and there are NO behaviour problems.
- The students are proactive, independent and use their initiative.
- They lead the class and proactively deal with any negativity.

Look, I don't want to sell you a pipe dream. Your students are humans like you. This is a very fluid idea, and your students are not fixed across the board. Some students can be disruptive in one subject and fully engaged in another. I have regularly seen students go from being absolute terrors to lovely little angels because they had a different teacher covering their lesson.

This can be daunting, especially if you have classes full of Disrupters and Compliants. Of course, your ultimate goal would be to get all your students to the Engaged level. But that's a dream. That could take years for you to do with every single class that you teach.

My first book was designed to help you take your students a couple of levels up the mountain so that you could do what you signed up for – teach. But after almost four years of running workshops, doing research, talking to teachers and being verbally assaulted (yes, it still happens to me too), I realised that some Disruptors are more challenging than others and needed a little more consideration.

This is where the next theory comes into play and will frame the rest of this book. So, let's see if we can tame our loveable rogues together, shall we?

THE FLASHPOINT TRIANGLE

Using the 'Trust Mountain' theory, we can look at practical ways to stop these 'Disruptors' from destroying your classes. Disruptors will either start or be involved in most flashpoint situations. Flashpoint situations stop learning, create drama, and make your classroom a horrible place to be in. Therefore, we want to stop the beef and make a strictly vegan atmosphere in our classrooms.

The Anatomy of a Flashpoint

In Fire Prevention training, we are taught that three essential elements must come together to create an inferno. They are:

- Oxygen
- Heat
- Fuel

The premise is simple: if you remove just one of those elements, a fire will not happen. So, while our lovely little cherubs cannot be compared to an elemental force of nature, flashpoints are remarkably similar in how they occur – and this has led me to develop my new theory, called 'The Flashpoint Triangle'.

A Flashpoint needs three elements to come together, which are:

- Escalation
- Hostility/Disengagement
- Audience

If you can take one of those elements out, you don't have a flashpoint. So, let's go through them one by one.

1) Escalation

Escalation is the 'fuel' of our triangle.

When a flashpoint situation starts, an invisible timer hangs ominously over the disagreement. Disruptors, by their nature, are more prone to become 'emotionally dysregulated' – in other words, these young people can go from being bubbly and happy to rampaging rage monsters in a New York minute. Therefore, you will have to learn how to quickly tamp down the confrontation before it blows up in your face.

2) Hostility/Disengagement

Hostility/disengagement is the 'heat' of our triangle.

You have a problem if you have a student who is hostile towards you. You have an even bigger problem if you have a student who refuses to engage with you and doesn't acknowledge you exist. This is the first and most frustrating stumbling block any teacher faces.

There's a saying in marketing that states people will only buy from companies that 'they know, like and trust'. It's exactly the same in teaching. You are selling them the idea that you are someone worthy to be listened to, respected and trusted. If you cannot get over that hurdle, there will be almost nothing that you will do to get them onside. Every lesson will be the equivalent of getting a root canal on your molars – painful, costly and ultimately miserable.

3) Audience

The audience is the 'oxygen' of our triangle.

Humans are social creatures – we tend to behave differently when in crowds versus when we are alone. It's encoded in our DNA and Apple/Android don't have an update. Emotions are infectious, and a wrong move on your part can turn a slight disagreement into a huge uproar. Remember that your students are watching and ranking your leadership ability when managing your classroom. If they perceive you as weak or unjust, you will create future problems down the line.

REFLECTION QUESTIONS

1. Think of a time that you had a severely disruptive student in your classroom. Before it all kicked off, can you remember what happened before the incident? In hindsight, could this have been prevented if something had been done differently?

2. If you deal with the same disruptive student regularly, what element of the Flashpoint Triangle mostly matches their behaviour? Are they downright hostile to you? Do they tend to escalate situations dramatically? Do they play up to the crowd?

3. How do you feel in the moment when you deal with Disruptors? Do you feel scared? Anxious? Apathetic? How do you feel after the episode? Does it take you a while to soothe yourself? Do you find yourself at home or in your downtime thinking about these incidents?

PRACTICAL TIPS

1. If you regularly deal with severely disruptive students and haven't established a robust self-care routine, you risk your emotional, physical and mental health. I won't mince my words here – I am writing this book because I genuinely care about great teachers like you who have to deal with the incredible demands of post-Covid teaching. According to TES, 44% of teachers in the UK will quit the profession over the next five years[2]. That's nearly half our workforce voting with their feet. Although over the course of this book, I give you a delightful assortment of tips and tricks to help you tame these students, it starts with you. You are just as worthy of the care you expertly give these students. Establish a self-care routine that restores your mental, emotional and physical health and stick with it.*

2. If you have persistent Disruptors who wreck your class, please do not feel that you are alone. Get your school's pastoral team involved. Obviously, the structure and look of the pastoral team will depend on the key-stage that you teach, but there should be a designated person who deals with pastoral issues. They are an absolute goldmine of knowledge and information, and can save you in a pickle. Find them and recruit them into your behaviour management squad.**

3. No matter what types of students you have in your class, you must communicate your expectations and set the ground rules off the bat. In a later chapter, I will walk you through how trauma can affect the mental health of your students and how students with Social Emotional and Mental Health needs (SEMH) may

behave 'poorly' to gain your attention. But regardless, you must go through the school's policy (or your own) to clearly define the boundaries that you will ALL follow. It doesn't have to be a massive showdown either – you can gather the class together and gently walk them through what they would like to see in the classroom. You can ask them, "How would you want everyone to be treated and why is that important?" and write their suggestions on the board. It is essential to get 'buy-in' from your students. If you can get them not only to understand WHAT the rules are but WHY they should follow them, then you are quids in. And if you're good, you can do this in 5 minutes.***

Let's boldly go into the 'Escalation' chapter like no other educators have gone before.

* For practical advice, check out the "Are You Taking Care of Your Engine?" chapter in AHT1.

** To know who to recruit into your squad, check out the "Assemble Your Team" chapter in AHT1.

*** For a practical step-by-step framework, check out "The Rules vs The Social Contract" chapter in AHT1.

ESCALATION

ESCALATION INTRODUCTION

As we learnt from the 2022 Oscars, things can go 'left' very quickly.

Like the drama we saw between Chris Rock and Will Smith, all it can take is the wrong comment, gesture or look, and everything around you can come crashing down instantly. So, make sure you keep people's names out of your mouth.

The critical actions you take at the start of a flashpoint can be the difference between a teachable moment with minimal disruption or a full-on classroom war.

This section will give you a whistle-stop tour of the latest mental health statistics regarding the UK's young people and what that means for your classrooms. First, you will learn what SEMH is and look at the factors that cause these challenges. Next, you will learn how to nurture your more vulnerable SEMH learners and how to build rapport with them despite any challenges they present. Finally, you will learn how to use psychological tricks with language to change your student's emotional state in a flash to help them focus on your lessons.

You will have a delightful buffet of tools to keep it mellow and peachy in your classroom.

Let's crack on.

YOUNG PEOPLE AND MENTAL HEALTH
PART 1: THE FACTS AND THE THEORIES

Have you ever been in this scenario? You've been dealing with a young person, things are going well, and either you or someone else says something banal or innocuous. Then, all of a sudden, the young person explodes with rage, swears at you and storms off, leaving you scratching your head, wondering what you did wrong – it's really confusing, right?

This was my everyday struggle when I was a NEETs Coordinator and later, an Alternative Provision Lead. We all get bad days – that's just being human. But hopefully, we (as adults) have learnt how to emotionally regulate ourselves and respond appropriately to things that annoy, scare and irritate us. If we walked around punching people in the face like Mike Tyson, we would quickly have our freedom relieved from us.

But some of our young people may not have had the adults or the guidance that can help them navigate these difficult emotions.

As I mentioned in the starting chapter, at this time of writing, the world seems to have turned upside-down and uncertainty has crept into our classrooms. Reduced mental health services and the creeping cost-of-living crisis add more pressure to families, negatively impacting our young people's mental health. Trust me, if your student is worried about whether they will be homeless next week because Daddy got sacked and Mum's been signed off sick with stress, you can't blame them for not being interested in Romeo's soliloquy in Act 5, Scene 5.

Young people's mental health challenges are real, they are on the rise, and we cannot ignore them any longer.

Young People's Mental Health: A Snapshot

According to a series of reports from Young Minds, a UK-based charity specialising in young people's mental health, our students have suffered considerably during the COVID pandemic and subsequent lockdowns. From their 2021 survey, they found[i]:

- One in six children aged five to 16 were identified as having a probable mental health problem in July 2021; a huge increase from one in nine in 2017. That's five children in every classroom (i).
- 83% of young people with mental health needs agreed that the coronavirus pandemic had worsened their mental health (iii).
- Less than 1 in 3 children and young people with a diagnosable mental health condition get access to NHS care and treatment.

That is terrifying. Those five students in every classroom with mental health challenges will probably be diagnosed with Social, Emotional, and Mental Health difficulties (SEMH.) According to semh.co.uk, SEMH is defined as "a specific category of SEN (Special Educational Need) that relate to the support a child might need to manage their emotions and behaviour... Often, these barriers to learning may be seen as a choice by others, and (subsequently) responses and approaches focus on sanctions and rewards rather than meeting the unmet need a behaviour may be communicating[2]."

Let's break it down further:

Social - refers to our student's ability to communicate with others and develop positive relationships.

Emotional - refers to their ability to appropriately process and manage their emotions in pro-social ways.

Mental Health - refers to their mental well-being, sense of self-worth, and how they see themselves fitting into society. These children may suffer from self-esteem issues and feelings of worthlessness that, if left unchecked, will have catastrophic effects on their entire life.

What Causes SEMH Needs in the First Place?

According to research, several possible reasons are particularly pertinent if they occur during childhood.

- Biological - how their mental and physical abilities are dictated by their unique genetic makeup.
- Attachment history - how their caregivers nurtured and reared these children affect how they form relationships with others.
- Trauma history - domestic violence, abuse, neglect, bullying, violent crime, social exclusion, hate, prejudice, and loss can have a detrimental impact on their development.

- Current family dynamics - if they live in a dysfunctional family system where their needs are being ignored, this can arrest their development. This could mean taking on roles beyond their stage of maturity, i.e. being a carer to a drug-addicted parent, or trying to appease an emotionally-abusive parent.

Many times, these students are survivors of horrendous circumstances, and thus they sadly may develop maladaptive ways to cope with these traumas.

But because they cannot emotionally regulate themselves, they are labelled as 'naughty children', which further blights them and their life chances.

SEMH and the Law

Thankfully, the Department for Education recognises how these difficulties will disadvantage these poor children and have created codes of conduct to help education institutions provide the best care for these students.

Now, I warn you, I'm going to have to get a bit more 'scholarly' in tone as I am dealing with official Government documents – but I'm going to do the best I can to break it down like faulty IKEA bunk beds.

<u>First question:</u> **What is the SEND Code of Practice?**

The SEND Code of Practice 2014 is statutory guidance for organisations that work with and support children and young people with special educational needs and disabilities. The Department for Education (DfE) created a set of guidelines that local authorities and schools should follow.

Second question: What are the essential requirements the document stipulates?

Good question. The whole document is a must-read for all educators, but I will try my best to boil down the most essential parts of the text as it pertains to SEMH learners.

In the UK, a fundamental law called the Equality Act 2010 protects people from discrimination in workplaces, schools and the wider society. Every discrimination law that the UK ever produced was bundled into this Act and made it illegal to discriminate against anyone's personal traits, which they call 'characteristics'. These include race, age, gender assignment, religion, sexual orientation and many others.

This Act underpins the guidance that schools and educational institutions must follow. In the SEND Code 2014, paragraph xix (19) on page 16 states the following[3]:

(Bear with me, I need to get my reading glasses out, it's a long paragraph...)

- They (schools and education institutions) must not directly or indirectly discriminate against, harass or victimise disabled children and young people.
- They must not discriminate for a reason arising in consequence of a child or young person's disability.

- They must make reasonable adjustments, including the provision of auxiliary aids and services, to ensure that disabled children and young people are not at a substantial disadvantage compared with their peers. This duty is anticipatory – it requires thought to be given in advance to what disabled children and young people might require and what adjustments might need to be made to prevent that disadvantage.

Third question: Are disabilities only physical?

Of course not.

According to UK Government guidance...[4]

- A mental health condition is considered a disability if it has a long-term effect on your normal day-to-day activity. This is defined under the Equality Act 2010.
- Your condition is 'long term' if it lasts, or is likely to last, 12 months.

So, here's the deal: the same way that we must make reasonable adjustments for students with physical/visible challenges (i.e. wheelchair users) is the same way we must make adjustments for students with SEN/SEMH needs.

You can help stop this vicious cycle.

In the next chapter, we will examine the power of relationships and why that is the key to helping our SEMH students overcome their limitations.

Let's stop here and do some reflecting:

REFLECTION QUESTIONS

1. Do you have SEMH students in your classroom? Have they been formally diagnosed? If so, have you read their statements or spoken to the appropriate adults to ensure that you understood what they needed?

2. How often do you communicate about the needs of your SEN/SEMH students in your school? Is this a regular occurrence, or does this happen occasionally? Would you have the opportunity to squeeze anything related to mental health into your everyday lessons?

3. Do you personally know anyone who has been diagnosed with SEMH? How was their schooling experience? How were they treated then, and what impact did it have on their life going forward?

PRACTICAL TIPS

I have only one tip for you in this section, and it's to read as much as you can around the subject. I know some academic texts are mind-numbingly dull, but there are still some great books for you to read! I am going to list my favourite texts, and I'm going to give you some 'left-field' book recommendations too – these books will not only help you with SEMH students but tricky individuals at work and in life. Thank me later.

School-Centric Reading

1. *The SEND Code of Practice 2014* by the Department for Education – I know it is not the most entertaining read, but it does a great job explaining the Government's rationale on how to deal with these SEMH challenges in schools, and it helps you understand the bigger picture. Let's look at the positives: it's free and it's on the Government's website. So, read it then go back to watching *Better Call Saul*.

2. *Nurture Groups in School: Principles in Practice* by Marjorie Boxall and Sylvia Lucas – This book is essential for anyone interested in SEMH. Boxall was an educational psychologist and a pioneer in SEMH pedagogy for fifty years until she died in 2004. Her work lives on through the 'Boxall Profile' – a checklist designed to identify the unmet needs of SEMH children and recommend how to address them. This book gives you the 'lay of the land' regarding SEMH and a solid grounding in creating environments to stabilise these students.

3. *When The Adults Change* by Paul Dix – Paul's work is lauded by schools up and down the country. Paul's whole system is driven by creating positive relationships with the students you teach by creating strategies that build rapport yet establish firm boundaries. It's a brilliant book for any teacher to have on their bookshelf.

4. *The Action Hero Teacher* by yours truly. So, you really didn't think I was not going to add my own book to this list? Really?!?

NON-SCHOOL-CENTRIC READING

While these books might not be for school teachers, they have been invaluable in helping me build relationships and understand the innate drives of my students (and other humans).

1. *How To Win Friends and Influence People* by Dale Carnegie – This book was written almost ninety years ago, but much of the advice is timeless. Some people might be put off by its folky and wholesome tone, but it holds many universal truths about building positive relations with others. I thoroughly recommend it.

2. *The Laws of Human Nature* by Robert Greene – This book is an absolute masterpiece on understanding human beings. Greene is almost the opposite of Carnegie, willing to delve deeper into the human psyche and reveal our darker and less noble sides to our nature. But this book highlights the subconscious drives that are not obvious to the untrained eye but dominate most of our social interactions, and gives you a roadmap on how to deal with difficult or complex characters. It's an absolute must-read.

3. *The Obstacle is The Way* by Ryan Holiday – Ryan Holiday is Robert Greene's protégé and is a master communicator, advising global companies on how to enhance their brands. In this book, he uses the philosophies of stoicism to help you deal with the trials and tribulations of modern life. Although it doesn't help you build relationships with people per se, it helps you look at negative things that may happen to you through different lenses and look for the advantage in the situation – which is incredibly handy when dealing with disruptive students! It will help you keep calm and become more strategic in dealing with challenges in your life. It's a 5 out of 5 for me!

YOUNG PEOPLE AND MENTAL HEALTH PART 2: RELATIONSHIPS ARE THE KEY TO DEALING WITH SEMH STUDENTS AND HERE'S WHY

Attachment Theory and Why it's Important in Your Classrooms

John Bowlby (1907-1990) was a British psychoanalyst who was the first to develop what we now refer to as 'attachment theory'. Building off Sigmund Freud's work, psychoanalysts try to help patients by exploring their emotions and highlighting their unconscious drives, which may be causing them distress.

For the record, I'm going to give you a very slim-downed version of his theory – I know some of you psychology post-grads might be spitting out your tea and throwing your crumpets out of the window! But our aim is to grasp the theory to better inform our teaching practice.

What is attachment?

Simply put, attachment is the deep emotional bond formed between the child and the caregiver from birth. This is critical to help the child develop physically and emotionally. According to Bowlby, infants have an innate drive to attach to a caregiver because it is vital to their survival. If the attachment bond fails to develop, the child will likely die.

Bowlby believed that between the moment of birth and roughly five-years-old was the most critical time for this attachment to form. But here's the kicker: Bowlby believed that the primary attachment created the template for all other relationships going forward. He wrote, "It is evident, however, that attachment behaviour is in no way confined to children. Although usually less readily aroused, we see it also in adolescents and adults... whenever they are anxious or under stress[5]."

In the 1970s, American-Canadian psychoanalyst Mary Ainsworth (1919-1999) significantly expanded Bowlby's theory. Through a series of careful experiments exploring how children reacted when separated from their primary caregiver, Ainsworth identified what she called 'attachment styles'. Her work radically changed our understanding of how early childhood experiences could affect how we relate to others in later life.

Here are the four main patterns she identified[6].

1) Secure Attachment

When separated from their parents, securely-attached children would get visibly upset and irritable. However, when their parents returned, they would be pleased to see them. When the parents went to comfort them, their attempts were fully accepted by the children. Although they could be soothed by strangers, they preferred their primary caregivers. The children knew they could rely on their parents to provide reassurance, security, and support.

Further studies revealed that as these children matured, they tended to be more empathetic to the needs of others, could concentrate for extended periods, and were less disruptive than others with non-secure attachment patterns. As they became adults, these individuals could foster trusting, reciprocal relationships, have higher self-esteem, and seek social support when needed.

In a perfect world, this would be the ideal situation we want for our children. But it doesn't always happen. Also, this is not to blame the caregivers as well – many factors can negatively affect a child's attachment, which sadly could be out of the carers' control, like grief, poverty and illness.

Let's explore the other styles.

2) Ambivalent Attachment

These children tended to be highly suspicious of strangers and were considerably distressed when their caregivers left. Unfortunately, when the parent did return, they tended not to be reassured or soothed by the caregiver. In some cases, the child will refuse comfort from the parent or could physically attack the parent.

Research suggests that as these children mature, they become very wary of getting close to others and are anxious about whether their loved ones truly care about them. This anxiety makes them emotionally push people away because they would rather cut off others before they could do it to them. Ironically, these individuals with ambivalent attachments may feel very distraught about their relationships ending, making them want to withdraw more, worsening the cycle.

3) Avoidant Attachment

Children with this attachment style proactively avoid caregivers; this pattern becomes even worse the longer the responsible adult is out of the picture.

These kids might not reject attention from a caregiver, but they might not actively seek it either, and they show no preference between their carers or a complete stranger.

Research suggests that these children grow into adults who find it challenging to form close relationships and foster any form of intimacy. They don't invest much emotion into their relationships and, when they end, don't seem to experience any distress. They avoid feelings of vulnerability and may find it challenging to communicate their thoughts and feelings. They also may find it difficult to support others emotionally, particularly through difficult times.

4) Disorganised-Insecure Attachment

These children often do not have a clear attachment style and can fluctuate between being needy, standoffish and avoidant. These children appear confused about how to deal with their carer and the other adults that may be able to help them.

Research suggests that this attachment style may form in a child whose primary caregiver switches from being a figure of reassurance to a figure of terror, and this unpredictability overwhelms the kid.

Studies conclude these children grow into adults with poor emotional regulation – going to extremes of behaviour like extreme happiness to sadness in a short time, which can make their relationships very volatile. They may also want to be extremely close to people, but because of their childhood experiences, they may push people away for fear of abandonment. They may also suffer from low self-esteem, which sadly may negatively affect their mental health and ability to thrive in their personal and professional lives.

Let's set the record straight: when looking at the things that I have mentioned in this chapter, it can be easy to assume that if a child comes from a wealthy background or from a particular demographic, class or race, they would be insulated from these specific problems, right? Hold your horses.

Although things like a higher socio-economic status can give you more opportunities to prevent these problems, it's not a guarantee these attachments won't be damaged. We have all seen enough news reports about celebrities, politicians and aristocrats to remind us that being stinkin' rich might make you a stinkin' parent.

Having a happy, trauma-free childhood is a true blessing and privilege. But, as Alain De Botton, the founder of 'The School of Life' lamented, "True privilege is an emotional phenomenon. It involves receiving the nectar of love – which can be stubbornly missing in the best-equipped mansions and oddly abundant in the bare rooms of modest bungalows[7]."

These attachment styles may help explain why your students act in specific ways and give clues on how to help them in our classrooms.

What does the future look like for SEMH children?

Honestly, it doesn't look good.

According to Unlocking Potential, a specialist charity that supports SEMH students[8]:

- By the age of 20, only 30% of adults diagnosed with SEMH needs at school have gained any qualifications.
- 99% of SEMH students do not make the national average academic progress of their peers.

Students with SEMH needs that are not met are more likely to:

- Develop substance abuse problems.
- Get stuck in unemployment/under-employment.
- Be exploited physically, mentally and sexually.
- Are more likely to not complete their GCSEs and become a NEET (Not in Employment Education or Training).

But even more tragically...

According to the Timpson Report 2019[9], which looked at the impact of school exclusions, there were two interesting findings:

- 46.7% of excluded children have SEN and SEMH needs.
- In a 2014 case study, over 60% of young people accessing youth justice services presented with speech, language and communication needs.

This tragic spiral has been dubbed:

'The School to Prison Pipeline'

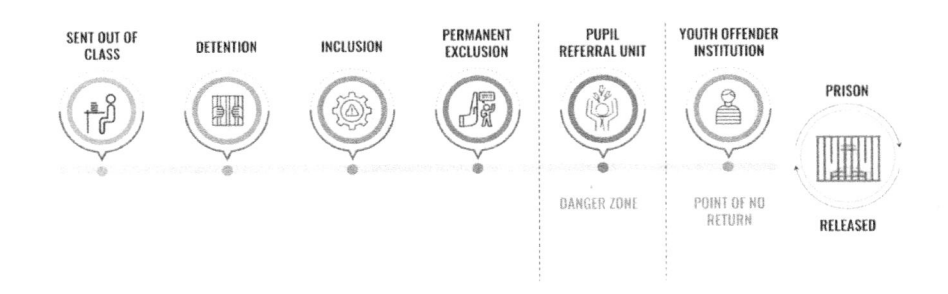

SENT OUT OF CLASS	DETENTION	INCLUSION	PERMANENT EXCLUSION	PUPIL REFERRAL UNIT	YOUTH OFFENDER INSTITUTION	PRISON
				DANGER ZONE	POINT OF NO RETURN	RELEASED

Another concerning government statistic is that over 90% of youth offenders in custody have been recorded as being persistently absent in school[10].

So, is it all doom and gloom? Should we just pack it in? Hell no! Let's reflect and look at what we can do in practice.

REFLECTION QUESTIONS

1. Since you have started teaching post-COVID (or interacting with your young people), have you noticed an adverse change in their behaviour and outlook? For example, do your students seem more irritable/anxious/unsure? How do you soothe them or help them with their concerns?

2. How have you responded if students have displayed signs of emotional distress in your classroom? Have you received training on how to help students with mental health challenges? Do you know who to signpost these students to if they persistently struggle to cope in your classroom?

3. Now that you have heard about 'the School to Prison Pipeline', do you feel it accurately portrays our education system for troubled students? What are your thoughts on excluding students who do have severe SEMH needs? How do you draw the line between genuine educational needs and destructive behaviour?

PRACTICAL TIPS

1. Don't take it personally – when you deal with SEMH students presenting challenging behaviour, it's easy to take it personally and think you are a terrible teacher. It can be extremely easy to actively dislike (or worse) the young people you are dealing with. I put my hands up on this one – I still fall into that trap. But please don't be hard on yourself. Guess what – you are human. Hopefully, this chapter will help you understand that it's not you most of the time. Some of these kids have been through absolutely horrific experiences and you're the poor adult who bears the brunt of it. Sadly, for some of our learners, if they tried to initiate that behaviour with their primary caregiver, it could lead to disastrous consequences. I am not excusing their behaviour in the slightest – we'll talk about that in a bit. But I realise that some teachers punish themselves when things go wrong and put it on their shoulders when that kid kicks off in their classroom. Please don't. I hope this simple fact can help you feel better. Make sure that you are looking after yourself, sanction where necessary, and when it's time to switch off, you bloody do. Your family, friends and loved ones need you too!

2. Recognise 'baselines' – no, I am not talking about anything to do with Craig David (for the record, I absolutely love Craig David – *7 Days* is a jam!), but you must make sure you know the students you teach. Everyone has a natural 'baseline' in their personality, and we usually don't tend to stray too far from our emotional 'setpoint'. Optimistic people tend to remain optimistic, cranky people tend to stay cranky, and so on. It's imperative to recognise

that if a child acts out of character for a significant period, we check in on them to establish that everything is OK. For example, if you teach a really bubbly child and they become withdrawn and sullen for two weeks, you must check in with that kid. You never know. You could be saving their life.

3. Another small but highly effective tip I learnt is what I call my 'two-minute check-ins'. After I set the main activity and have the students working independently, I walk around the class and simply ask them how their day was. I would always try to include something personal (but light) in the conversation to see if they were OK. These were the examples of questions I would ask:

"How did your sister's exam go last week?"

"I hope you don't feel too bad about Chelsea losing on the weekend."

"Did you get the chance to watch the new Avengers film you were telling me about? How did you find it?"

"Congratulations on getting 100 merits! You must be really proud – well done!"

Although this is incredibly simple to do, never underestimate the power of a two-minute check-in. For the reasons I explained in this chapter, you might be the only stable adult relationship in this young person's life. Even the coldest learner will melt if they persistently see that you are taking an interest in their life and wellbeing.

Although this may seem like common sense, some teachers still don't do this. Yes, it involves you learning about your students but look at this as a long-term investment. Your children will learn to trust you as the relationship develops, and in turn, they will want to work for you and be more likely to follow your instructions. No one will care how much you know until they know how much you care.

LEARN TO BE 'RUDE': USE PATTERN INTERRUPTS TO TAKE CONTROL OF TRICKY CONVERSATIONS

Folks, I am sure like me, you heard a lot of these phrases from your parents growing up.

"Don't eat with your mouth open."

"Hold the door open for others."

"Always say please and thank you."

"Be kind."

"Use your inside voice."

"Sit up straight."

And so on. That's absolutely fine. But for this chapter, I will ask you to do something slightly different. I will challenge you to be rude to your kids.

OK, calm down (I know an SLT member out there who panicked when I said that! Lol!).

But it's not in the way that you think. So, just bear with me, and by the end of this chapter, I will equip you with a clever, little 'Jedi mind trick' that may help you tackle and de-escalate some of your trickier conversations.

What are 'Patterns'?

Before we define a 'pattern interrupt', let's first look at what a 'pattern' is. In this case, another name we can use for a pattern is a 'habit'. A habit, in psychology, is any regularly repeated behaviour that requires little or no thought and is learned rather than innate[11].

You see, humans are creatures of habit. As brilliant as our brains are, they quickly get worn out when they have to constantly process new information. So, our brains developed a nifty trick: if they're repeatedly presented with the same situation, your brain produces new neural connections dedicated to completing that task. As you repeat that task, that neural 'road' gets broader and deeper, moving from the 'thinking' part of our brain into the deeper structures of the organ attached to our nervous system.

If this continues, this task or activity becomes second nature, and we don't have to think about it, freeing up valuable resources to think of other things. Patterns go for our verbal interactions too. Anything that gets repeated gets learnt – or as a neural scientist would say, 'neurons that fire together, wire together.'

In my late teens, every session of learning to drive absolutely exhausted me. First, learning to focus on the road while knowing when to work the clutch, the gearstick and the accelerator boggled my brain. But as the years rolled on, it's become so innate that I can talk to my child in the backseat, listen to music, and drive on a motorway seemingly without thinking. Driving no longer taxes me; thank goodness for that – life is stressful enough!

Although scientists and researchers haven't agreed, many estimate that 40-70% of what we do daily is through these patterns. For example, have you ever travelled somewhere familiar (usually work) and can't remember how you got there? Yep, your brain followed your 'travel pattern' and took you along for the ride.

Patterns don't always have to be positive: sadly, this exact mechanism in our brain is responsible for creating destructive addictions that wreak havoc on our lives, such as alcoholism, drug addiction, workaholism and many more. As we're doing now, we break our patterns by bringing awareness to them.

Your Secret Weapon: The 'Pattern Interrupt'

OK, so I know you are thinking: "That sounds great Karl, but how is it relevant to my classroom?" Think about it: we can get stuck in specific patterns of interaction that don't help us. Don't believe me? Let's look at the most common dialogue pattern in human society. When a stranger greets you, this is the usual dialogue:

Stranger: "*Hi - How are you?*"

You: "*I'm fine, thanks.*"

99% of the time, you will respond with "I'm fine", even if your partner left you, your cat died, your house is on fire, and you were being hunted by the CIA for a crime you didn't commit. If we said any of those things to a stranger, it would be really awkward. This is an accepted pattern of civil society and we rarely break it.

If you teach a class long enough, you will get into familiar dialogue patterns with your students, and they can get quite frustrating. If you have a disruptive student who does something that you don't like, this could be the pattern you enter in: (Let's call this pattern the "Negative Student-Teacher Pattern" for future reference)

- He misbehaves
- You nag
- He protests
- You shout
- He gets verbally abusive
- You send him out
- He gets a detention
- You phone home
- He steps into your lesson the next day and does something wrong

And repeat ad infinitum – this is exhausting and frustrating and slows down learning time, leaving you regretting your career choices. This is where 'pattern interrupts' come in. A pattern interrupt is "a way to alter a person's mental, emotional, or behavioural state to break their typical habits. Think of it as an unexpected act that jolts them into another state of mind[12]."

It sounds complicated but salespeople, illusionists and comedians use pattern interrupts to help sell, astound and entertain us. A great pattern interrupt allows us to look at something that we take for granted in a new way and change negative interactions into positive ones.

Before I give you the list of my favourite pattern interrupts, it's important to note that pattern interrupts are best used *before* things escalate out of control. If you have a student frothing at the mouth in rage, these pattern interrupts would probably aggravate the student more.

I tend to use pattern interrupts when it's getting a little testy and tense, but the conversation is still somewhat civil. Some of these pattern interrupts may seem random, funny or bonkers, but the aim is the same: to steer the conversation away from a flashpoint and into something that can be resolved quickly.

Here are my favourites, and I am sure you will find one that will tickle your fancy.

1) The Super Detailed Pattern Interrupt

Teacher: "*John, please stop talking while I'm teaching.*"

John: "*I just had to tell Michael something.*"

Teacher: "*Let me guess, you were going to tell Michael that on the Friday, 22nd November, 1963, John F Kennedy was assassinated in Dallas, Texas while riding in a presidential motorcade through Dealey Plaza...*"

A firm favourite. You can use this to re-steer the lesson to your subject (like above) or any subject you want. If you know the student well and have a good relationship with them, you can use it to go into detail about what they were going to talk about. This will hopefully elicit a laugh and get the students back on track.

2) The 'Talk-To-Yourself' Pattern Interrupt

Your student, Sarah, enters the classroom late and fails to acknowledge you.

Teacher: (Playing both parts)

"Sorry Sir I am late."
"Why are you late?"
"Because I had to go to the toilet."
"Please don't do that again and open the textbook to page 223."

I know it sounds bonkers, but this can be incredibly effective, especially when you have a student that tends to not respond well to you. Ham up the acting but don't be disrespectful. Try to be comedic to get the maximum effect. I use this when I want to gently remind students of their manners.

3) The Visual Pattern Interrupt

I once heard a story of a Maths teacher who placed a replica human skull on his desk at the start of a tricky class, to his pupils' bemusement. He told his students that it would be 'important' to the topic, and they needed to listen to get clues on how the skull would help them understand the lesson. They focused intently, trying to unravel the mystery. The baffled students racked their brains, trying to think of how the skull connected with trigonometry, but there were no connections. At the end of the lesson, the teacher set the homework, picked up the skull and left. Here's the hilarious thing: there wasn't any connection at all. He used the skull to get them to focus on what he was teaching and minimise the disruption, which worked.

The key with this technique is to bring in an item, a piece of clothing or a prop that is out of the blue and will pique your students' curiosity, and it would be even better if it connects to your subject. But don't take it too far – if you bring in something inappropriate or outlandish, you will become the distraction, and it may land you in hot water with the higher-ups. Apply a little common sense.

4) The 'Godfather' Pattern Interrupt

This pattern interrupt is fun! This came from a story about movie star Bruce Willis. As Bruce started to produce more films, he often found himself in noisy rooms, full of power-hungry producers and actors shouting over each other to get attention. So, Bruce decided he would do the opposite and became quieter, spoke less and took long pauses before he replied. He started to talk in near-whispers, forcing the others in the room to quiet down and focus on what he was saying.

If you want to ooze authority, learn to still yourself, speak calmly and firmly and draw attention to yourself by your presence. Constantly screaming and shouting will show that you are not in control of that situation, and your students may learn to ignore it. I call this the 'Godfather' Pattern Interrupt after Marlon Brando's depiction of Vito Corleone in the first *Godfather* film. If you find yourself in a rowdy classroom, I know it sounds counterproductive, but talk softer, have relaxed body language, a neutral face and say fewer words. Eventually, your students will realise that you want their attention, and most will fall silent. Another fictional person who did this brilliantly was the villain Gus

Fring in hit TV show *Breaking Bad*, whose mysterious, sphinx-like demeanour terrified the other characters in the drama. For the record, I do not condone any of Fring's activities! However, it has worked very well for me to this day – try it!

5) The Question-Answer Pattern Interrupt

This is a slight variation of the 'Talk-To-Yourself' pattern, which is a little more assertive – I usually use this when a student is trying to engage in an argument, and it needs to be shut down quickly before it escalates. For example:

Teacher: "*What should you be doing?*"
Matthew: "*I should....*"
Teacher: "*Look at the board and write down the first question.*"

I tend to use this pattern interrupt if the more playful ways don't work. The firmer tone should indicate to the student that they are crossing a line. A word of caution: if you have extremely disruptive students, this approach could backfire on you. Use this technique sparingly.

6) The 'Change-The-Subject' Pattern Interrupt

This interrupt can steer a conversation that might get too awkward or sensitive. Although this is obvious, the key is how it is done. For example:

Meghan (who is in Year 11): "*Sir, last night, I watched* Bridgerton, *and the Duke of Hastings took Daphne into the bedroom and...*"

Teacher: "*Okaaayyyyy, what was the name of Duncan's wife, anyone?*"

If you do this harshly, this can quickly become a flashpoint situation. The dramatic exaggeration of the word 'OK' keeps it light-hearted, yet lets the student know that's an area you don't want to broach. They should get the message if you have a decent relationship with the student. A comedic exaggeration softens the blow – use it how you see fit.

7) The Confused Pattern Interrupt

Joseph shouts across the classroom while the teacher is speaking.

Joseph: "*Oi, Bob, gimme that pen now.*"

Teacher: "*Huh?*"

Joseph: "*Sorry Miss, I meant 'Bob, could you pass me that pen please? Thank you.*"

Ideally, this is where you want to get to. Although this is remarkably simple, a lot is happening in this interaction. The student knew the standards of the class and your reaction prompted him to remember how to treat his classmates, correct his behaviour and apologise for it. This also hints that he has a positive relationship with his teacher. Again, a little exaggeration for comedic effect can sweeten the message. If you master this skill, it can help you resolve many minor irritations and stop many arguments from escalating.

REFLECTION QUESTIONS

1. Do you feel you constantly 'nag' your students to get things done? When you do, how do your students respond? How do you feel after you have to go through this pattern?

2. Look at the 'Negative Student Teacher Pattern' again. How often do you face this? Monthly? Weekly? Daily? Is it with the same students, or are they always different? Are there any points in the pattern you feel you can now interrupt to get a positive outcome?

3. Have you ever faced a student you feel has the verbal 'upper hand' on you? Do they use their own pattern interrupts to disrupt your lessons? What will you do differently now you have learnt this technique?

PRACTICAL TIPS

1. I realise this might be a little 'out there' for some of you. Everyone is different, and I understand that these pattern interrupts are a little more difficult for some than others. However, I would still encourage you to try and adapt these techniques to your style. If I were to rank them, interrupts 1 and 4 would be the easiest to execute and if you master them, will significantly decrease flashpoint situations.

2. Remember, the main effect of pattern interrupts should be to 'lighten' engagements and not to humiliate your students. This skill has a dark side, and these techniques can fall into sarcasm, putting you into 'insult comic' territory (see the "Meet The Disruptors" chapter). Keep it light, and as wishy-washy as it sounds, hold your students in 'positive regard' and use these tools to build a positive relationship with them. Always use the 'Line Manager Test' – if you would not be happy to say it in front of your line manager, then you shouldn't say it at all. Also, if your students are being abusive, rude or disrespectful, don't get into a battle with them; follow your school's sanction protocol and follow through*.

3. If you are still unsure if you are doing it right, a great fictional example of a person using these techniques is Tony Stark, played by Robert Downey Jr in the Marvel Cinematic Universe's Avengers series. Downey's Iron Man carries himself like a person who is confident and doesn't take himself or the situations he literally lands in too seriously. Unless in extreme circumstances, he keeps his cool and delivers his communications in an assertive

yet light way. Please do not use his sarcasm but bring that same playful, relaxed spirit to these techniques, and you will be onto a winner.

* If you struggle with how to sanction, check out the "Sanction Quickly and Restore" chapter in AHT1.

MAKE 'EM SCARED TO LOSE: LEARN HOW TO USE NEGATIVITY IN A POSITIVE WAY

OK, time for some visualisation. You can close your eyes if you want – I'm not picky.

I want you to imagine that you're in a Las Vegas casino and looking fabulous, darling – like you just walked out of a 007 movie. You glance over and spot me in the distance on the crowded casino floor – the debonair croupier dishing out cards with a wink and a smile. You approach me with your swilled martini (or non-alcoholic beverage) and wait for the next round. I'm in a generous mood, so I give you £1,000 worth of chips to play with. Then I offer you a bet.

* Option 1: Take a gamble on the roulette table, and you have a 50% chance of **winning** £1,000 more.

* Option 2: Don't take the bet, and I will **definitely hand you £500.**

Which one would you pick? (Write down your answer – this will become important in a second...)

Answer _____

Let's say you've been doing well, and you're smashing the table. Now, you have £2,000 worth of chips in your hands. So, I have decided to offer you another bet.

*Option 1: Take a gamble, and you have a 50% chance of **losing £1,000**.

*Option 2: Don't take the chance and **definitely lose £500**.

Which one would you pick? (Again, write your answer down.)

Answer _____

OK, let's push the James Bond stuff to one side – a serious point must be made. These hypothetical questions were actually tested in a ground-breaking study by Daniel Kahneman and Amos Tversky in a 1979 paper called 'Prospect Theory: An Analysis of Decision under Risk'. Their report described how people make investment decisions around economic risk and discovered something very intriguing...

In a similar study, when presented with the first scenario, 84% of people chose Option 2: to take the £500 guaranteed win. However, when offered the second scenario, 69% decided to take Option 1, which was to gamble and take the chance to avoid the loss rather than taking the £500 hit.

What does this all mean? The guaranteed win in Scenario 1 and the guaranteed loss in Scenario 2 were £500 – so why did they get different outcomes? Their studies concluded that "people are willing to take on risk to avoid a loss, even when they're not willing to do the same for a gain[13]".

In their 1979 study, they highlighted the economic concept we know as 'loss aversion', which states that the pain of losing is psychologically twice as powerful as the pleasure of gaining. As a result, people are more willing to take risks (or behave dishonestly...) to avoid a loss than to make a gain[14]. Human beings hate to lose and soon you will understand why.

Why Amazon Reviews Can Ruin My Day

Initially, it took a while for AHT1 to build traction, but in the second year of publication, the reviews started to roll in on Amazon, and to my surprise, most of them were 5-star ratings. I was over the moon! So, all those late nights and early mornings were not in vain. It was all finally happening, or so I thought...

Then I got my first 3-star rating. I think it was the 18th review, and when I got the alert, I stared at the screen and was distraught. It knocked my perfect 5.0 out 5 to 4.7, and now that fifth star had a chunk missing. For the record, it's not because I thought so highly of myself that my book had to have the 'perfect score' – it's actually the opposite.

You see, readers, I have a little confession to make: writing my first book was a real struggle for me, and I felt like an imposter while writing it. Although I did OK in my GCSEs, I never had any experience writing a non-fiction book, and every time I sat down at my computer to type, I was constantly assaulted by negative thoughts in my mind like:

"What you write is absolute garbage – who do you think you are?"

"C'mon, Karl, you're just an inner-city London kid! You're not some high and mighty academic – why would anyone listen to you?"

"Remember when you tried that other project? It flopped! This one is going to flop too!"

"No one is going to read this book! This is such a waste of time!"

That 3-star review brought back all those negative voices, and I hated it.

Rather than focus on the 17 other people who gave AHT1 glittering reviews, that average review was the one I was ruminating about the most and bothered me for days.

Have you ever had this experience? Where you do something that opens you up to critique, and despite all the positive feedback you receive, one negative comment can deflate you? I'm not alone, right? This points to an interesting quirk in our psychology called 'negativity bias'.

What is Negativity Bias?

Human beings, in general, are hardwired for negativity. 'Negativity bias' has been defined as a cognitive bias "that results in adverse events having a more significant impact on our psychological state than positive events.[15]" Like with the money experiment, even if the positive and negative events carry the same weight, we tend to feel the loss more intensely than the win.

But how would that be helpful? From an anthropological point of view, it makes perfect sense. Your brain has one job: to keep you alive as long as possible. For our savannah-dwelling ancestors, their decisions carried more weight than our modern ones, like whether we should eat Nando's or KFC for dinner. Tierney and

Baumeister wrote in their book, *The Power of Bad*, "To survive, life has to win every day. Death has to win only once. A small error or miscalculation can wipe out all successes. The negativity bias is adaptive... (it's) a trait that improves the odds of survival for an individual or a group.[16]"

Huh, I hear you say – where are you going with this? How will being 'negative' help me teach my rowdy Year 9 Geography class? Great question – just hang on in there. For reasons that I will explain in more depth in the chapters "Group Dynamics 101" and "Help Them Make Better Decisions", our young students' thinking abilities are not as mature as ours. Young people overestimate the likelihood of succeeding or never getting caught in whatever ill-advised plan they are cooking. Their youth makes them believe they have a red cape and can leap tall buildings in a single bound... Apparently, us oldies "don't know anything".

In this case, we are using 'negativity bias' to help counter the disruptive behaviour, and our aim is to help the student become more grounded and aware of the consequences of their actions.

As an adult, it's your responsibility to help guide them and help them make better future decisions – and here's how.

The Easy Road and Hard Road Technique Revisited and Updated

In my first book, I wrote about a technique called 'The Easy Road and The Hard Road', which I believe is simply the best way to use 'negativity bias' for good. I will walk you through it step-by-step and highlight where using 'negativity bias' helps us correct poor behaviour.

I recommend using this technique when you can speak to the young person on a one-to-one basis or away from their peers. This can be done in 2 minutes or 20 – depending on the issue's severity. In this example, 'Katie' had a full-blown argument with 'Rebecca' in your classroom, and you had to step in before it became physical. They were sent away and they both agreed that Katie had started the argument. Katie has a 30-minute detention with you after school, but she is still unapologetic. Here are the steps:

1) Talk Calmly

This is absolutely critical. If you 'blow up' and scream at the student, you will most likely make them defensive, and with a Disruptor, you will start a flashpoint situation. Always remember: the calmest person in the room usually wins in a heated discussion. Be polite and ask them how they are feeling. The best way to do this is if you are both seated. Think about your body language: if possible, keep your face neutral and do not hover over the student or invade their space.

2) Present the Student with 2 Options: Minimise the Positive and Lean into the Negative

If you and the student are both calm and can have a reasonable dialogue, present your student with two options based on what happened in the class. One is the Easy Road – this is an opportunity to resolve the situation, whether it is an apology, following the procedure or correcting what went wrong. The other choice is the Hard Road, which will involve a negative consequence like a sanction. When explaining the choices, you want to gloss over any perceived positives that the student may feel and lean heavily into the negative ones that the situation will bring to activate the negativity bias. Here's an example:

"Katie, we agreed at the beginning of the term that we would listen and respect each other, but what happened with Rebecca disrupted the class. Although it might have felt good to shout the odds at Rebecca, you are in really serious trouble now. Look, the 'Easy Road' would be to apologise to Rebecca, and this detention will close the issue. If you can't do that Katie, you have chosen the 'Hard Road', meaning I will have to call home, speak to your Head of Year and escalate this process to the Deputy Headteacher. We have the Chessington trip planned for the end of term, and I know you and Shania have been looking forward to it. Don't let this spoil what you have spent a term working towards."

Notice what I did there? In sales, we call that 'pressing the pain points'. By walking through every single consequence in a calm, pragmatic, but empathetic way, you will be more likely to get Katie to reflect and think about her decisions. If you come in the room and scream, "KATIE, YOU MESSED UP-- YOUR CHESSINGTON TRIP IS OVERRRRRRRRRR!", you won't get the response that you desire.

3) Give Them the Chance to Make the Choice

The key to this strategy is choice. You have put the ball in the student's court. In doing this, you ask your student to take responsibility for their behaviour.

Another reason this is effective is that it gives a short time for the student to reflect on what is happening. Please also remember that students with SEMH difficulties may need a longer time to process this information as they are more prone to becoming emotionally dysregulated. Give. Them. Time. It's critical. After the time you set, come back and ask for their answer. If they don't answer or are defiant, they have chosen the Hard Road, and you must follow through with whatever sanctions or procedures you have in place.

How to be Negative About Yourself and Still be Positive

Here's another nifty trick you can do with 'negativity bias', which can help you foster positive relationships with tricky students. For example, some students are highly defensive and resistant. They may be used to being told off and sanctioned and no action seems to get them to engage. If you have faced this situation, negativity bias may hold the key to building those relationships – but you will have to turn that lens on yourself.

Yes, you heard me right. No, I haven't been smoking anything. Before you have that difficult conversation with that learner, I want you to consider all the things the student has against you and bring this up in your discussion. Yes, this may take some humility and cause discomfort, but the benefits outweigh the drawbacks.

In his brilliant book *Never Split The Difference*, former FBI negotiator Chris Voss calls this technique the 'Accusation Audit', which can be just as effective when negotiating with a violent terrorist as with a moody teen. Voss states that using this technique doesn't necessarily mean that you 'agree' with their view. Voss writes, "By acknowledging the other person's situation, you immediately convey that you are listening. And once they know that you are listening, they may tell you something you can use[17]." Let's use the Katie example again to show how this can work in a real-life situation:

"Look Katie, I know things haven't always been good between you and me in the classroom. I have been harsh with you in the past, and I tend to look at you when things go wrong in class. I know it must feel like all the teachers pick on you and try to make your life miserable. I'm sure it must be scary to face your GCSEs – maybe that's why you felt frustrated with Rebecca."

This shows that you are self-aware and willing to reflect on your behaviour, which can foster trust. It also demonstrates that you are self-confident and can admit your flaws, which helps the other person do the same.

And lastly, it helps clear up any misconceptions. In this example, Katie may tell you that Rebecca posted an offensive TikTok video about her that she didn't like – that's fine because it gives you new information that you may never have gotten if you didn't use that technique. As someone once said, "information changes situations". The more information you can get, the closer you are to a resolution.

REFLECTION QUESTIONS

1. When discussing poor behaviour with students, what is your approach? Are you aggressive, or are you cool, calm and collected? How has that gone in the past?

2. If you've ever had to conduct detentions yourself, how do you do them? Do you try to do any restorative work with them, or do you make them do nothing? If you have repeat offenders, how do they respond to you in those periods?

3. If you have a poor relationship with the same student, have you reflected on your contribution to that tension? If you have been at fault, have you been willing to talk to that student about it? If so, how did it go?

PRACTICAL TIPS

1. In teaching, I know time is at a premium. 'The Easy Road, Hard Road' technique can be used quickly. Make sure you display your classroom expectations/school rules and gently remind your students if they fall short. If they're repeat offenders, take them to one side, give a quick ultimatum using the ERHR technique and give them one minute to make up their minds. If they do not comply, sanction as necessary*.

2. I believe sanctions and detentions are perfect opportunities to do pastoral work and build rapport with your students. If you get 20 minutes where you can have that one-to-one time with them, by gosh, use it! That way, you can go deeper into the techniques I have described in this chapter. This is especially true if you have a student that is emotionally dysregulated, as they may need time to calm down (and you might need that time too**).

3. If you have done wrong to your student, please apologise. Sometimes we do things to hurt our students without even knowing it. It's easy to get defensive and believe we are inherently 'right' because of our position. Please be receptive if the student reveals that you are at fault after being willing to admit your transgressions. This is an opportunity to deepen your understanding of that student and hopefully a chance to help you and that student climb up Trust Mountain. After the apology, establish the next steps to avoid further misunderstandings in the future.

* If you want more information on the ERHR technique, check out the "Be Just, Firm and Fair" chapter in AHT1.

** If you find yourself constantly giving the same students sanctions, you may need a stronger intervention. Check out the "Interventions and Letting Go" chapter in AHT1.

DISENGAGEMENT/HOSTILITY

DISENGAGEMENT/HOSTILITY
INTRODUCTION

When you face a student who either ignores, belittles or verbally assaults you, it can feel like your whole world is caving in. These flashpoints spin in your mind for hours, leaving you shocked it escalated so quickly. Disengagement and hostility is the 'heat' of a flashpoint and the spark that starts the inferno.

Nobody gets into teaching to put up with this.

It's tough, but I got you.

In this section, you will learn about what it means to be a 21st Century classroom leader in a three-part series that will help you:

- ♦ Discover who you truly are and what hidden potential you may be hiding.
- ♦ Give you practical tips and tricks on how to be assertive yet approachable at the same time.
- ♦ Look at a case study analysing one of the greatest living football managers, Jürgen Klopp, and how he can help you in your classrooms.
- ♦ Lastly, I will 'pop the hood' and look at the nuts and bolts of where hostility and disengagement come from. You will learn about six different types of Disruptors, how to spot their tricks and how to deal with them in style!

You ready?

In the words of Jean-Luc Picard, 'Engage.'

THE LEADERSHIP ZONE PART 1 - THE PERSONA AND THE SHADOW: WHY YOU MUST GET TO KNOW THE REAL YOU

In my first book, I introduced another mental model called 'The Classroom Management Spectrum'. The model was simple: every teacher has a classroom management style that lies on a spectrum between 'authority' and 'warmth'.

In my first book, I described the three classroom management styles teachers must absolutely avoid to prevent their classes becoming warzones, which were:

A) **The Dictator** - All Authority, No Warmth.

B) **The Doormat** - All Warmth, No Authority.

C) **The Yo-Yo** - switches between being a Dictator and a Doormat in a short period.

To be an effective classroom manager, you had to be near the middle, which I dubbed 'The Leadership Zone'.

TOO MUCH AUTHORITY   BALANCED   TOO MUCH WARMTH

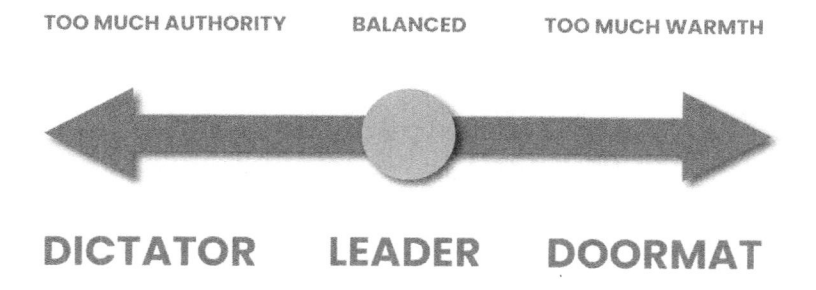

DICTATOR   LEADER   DOORMAT

Almost four years after writing *The Action Hero Teacher* and receiving feedback from educators, it became evident that many teachers struggle with getting the balance right, especially using 'authority'.

This bothered me: why are so many great teachers hamstrung by their own insecurities to lead? But through my research, I think I found the answer.

Carl Jung's Shadow and Persona

Carl Jung (1875-1961) was a 20th-Century psychotherapist and psychiatrist who created the field of analytical psychology. Amongst his ground-breaking theories were the concepts of the Persona, the Shadow and the Anima and Animus archetypes (don't worry – I'll explain them in a bit).

I'm not a qualified psychotherapist, but his ideas are worth touching on regarding how we carry ourselves in the real world.

The Persona

In terms of our personality, Jung believed that we developed a part of our character called the 'Persona'. This is the character that we display when we are in wider society.

As humans, our personas allow us to conform to certain expectations of the environments we find ourselves in, i.e. doctors will act more like doctors in a hospital, teachers will act more like teachers in a school and so on. This does not mean that you are fake. On the contrary, we need our personas to help us successfully navigate through civil society.

The Persona starts to develop in children around three to five-years-old, when they develop their own sense of self.

The Shadow

Around the same time that the Persona develops, another aspect of our character grows simultaneously and that's our 'Shadow'. The Shadow represents all the parts of ourselves that we see as less desirable – our impulses, desires, our less than noble thoughts, our baser instincts and what makes us feel guilty.

Also, Jung believed within our shadows lived the 'anima' and the 'animus', which are our personality's masculine and feminine aspects. Jung believed that the anima represented the latent female traits in men and the animus represented the latent male traits in women.

Now you might be thinking...

What the hell has this got to do with teaching?

Well, everything.

Your character construction is how 'You' show up in the world. This determines how people interact with you and the quality of your relationships.

Also, the Persona doesn't make you 'good', and the Shadow doesn't make you 'evil'. Jung believed people who over-identified with their personas were brittle, fake and inauthentic.

Not everything in the Shadow is 'bad'. Jung believed that the Shadow contained positive traits like assertiveness, creativity, wisdom and individuality. Those who constantly tried to repress their Shadows were at risk of 'shadow possession', which was a state where the Shadow would completely take over a person, often in destructive and unpredictable ways.

Jung believed that all humans should integrate all parts of their character to become a 'self'. If successful, this integration leads you to present the best version of yourself. Jung wrote, "People will do anything, no matter how absurd, in order to avoid facing their own souls... Because they cannot get on with themselves and have not the slightest faith that anything useful could ever come out of their own souls. That includes the parts of yourself that you may reject or not accept, like your failures and tragedies[1]."

Dear educator, you must know and analyse your character to see how you tick.

Obviously, this was an incredibly scant overview of Jung's work, and if you want to explore your subconscious, get a trained psychotherapist! But for those who struggle with getting the balance, try to see within yourself the opposite trait.

If you are too warm, you need to get more assertive (animus).

If you are too assertive, you need to get warmer (anima).

OK, that's the end of Part 1 – readers, you know what time it is. It's time to reflect.

REFLECTION QUESTIONS

1. Looking at the Classroom Management Spectrum, where do you think you sit? Are you one of the extremes (Dictator, Doormat or Yo-Yo)? When others observe your classes, what have they said about your behaviour management? Was it good or bad?

2. Do you feel that you can be authentic at work? If yes, how have you implemented this into your teaching practice? If not, why? What is holding you back from adding your personal magic to your teaching?

3. When you're feeling tired, stressed-out or irritated, how does that affect your teaching? Do you tend to lash out, or do you withdraw? When your limits are pushed, what things do you do to soothe yourself?

PRACTICAL TIPS

1. You must understand your classroom management style and understand that you have the power to change it. Your classroom management style will depend on the context in which you teach. If you teach in Alternative Provision, Pupil Referral Units (PRUs) or Youth Offenders institutions, you may have to lean a little more on your authority. If you teach in Early-Years or with students with severe SEN or physical challenges, you may lean a little more on your warmth. This zone may move around depending on the classes you teach in a single day! That's fine, if you do not stray too far from the centre. Balance is key.*

2. During your day, pay attention to when you're stressed, tired or ill, because this often points to the 'shadow' part of your personality. Many teachers (including myself) feel guilt or shame when we 'act out' in class. Of course, you must follow the Teaching Standards and the staff behaviour policies set by your school, and where possible, you apologise and rectify your mistake. But what I am trying to get at is that you must reflect and learn why you behaved in that manner, as it will give you clues on what you need to work on. For example, just say you screamed at a student and gave them a severe punishment. Then you reflect on your actions and think you may have gone too far. You then must go deeper and reflect on the core of your frustrations. Has this kid been getting on your nerves for weeks, and this was the final straw? Could you have dealt with the issues before you 'went bananas' in a better manner? Sometimes our resentments, fears and anxieties tell us there is something internally that we need to

deal with. Listen to your inner feelings and face your fears. Unfortunately, most of the time, the more you ignore a negative situation, the more it will grow and become worse to deal with. Don't delay, have the difficult conversations immediately so that the resentment doesn't multiply down the road.

3. If you constantly feel anxious, harassed, or at breaking point, this is a terrible sign. Look, our jobs are stressful, but it shouldn't be a constant battle to get out of bed every morning, especially when it comes to the behaviour of the students or adults that you work with. Our nervous systems were not built to be constantly on 'red alert' 24/7, 365 days of the year. These negative states of being are classic signs of burnout. Take it from me; as a person who has had burnout, you MUST increase your self-care, get the support you need at work from your mentor or line manager, and take drastic steps to preserve your health. You are no good to anyone if your health is gone. The longer you leave it, the worse it becomes, which could have catastrophic impacts on every area of your life. Look at ways to eat, rest better and perhaps look at how to ease your workload. No job is worth poor mental and physical health. Please look after yourself**.

* If you are still unsure what your behaviour management style is, read the "Avoid The Extremes" chapter in AHT1, which will have a mini-questionnaire and suggestions on what you need to work on.

** In AHT1, I have a whole chapter dedicated to self-care, "How Well Are You Managing Your Emotional Engine?" It goes in-depth on ensuring you are in tip-top physical and emotional condition for the classroom. So, have a look and follow the principles.

THE LEADERSHIP ZONE PART 2: HOW TO BUILD YOUR LEADERSHIP PERSONA

Develop 'Happy High Status'

This term was coined by best-selling author, broadcaster and media personality Viv Groskop in her book, *How to Own the Room: Women and the Art of Speaking*. Although she is talking about public speaking, this can easily apply to the classroom, because guess what? You are speaking in front of the public. Viv writes:

"This quality (Happy High Status) can't be faked. But it can be acquired, practiced and improved upon. Very close to charisma, it's true that some people have it naturally. They are the people we all gravitate towards in social situations because they make us feel comfortable.[2]"

People who display this trait are:

- Confident
- Charismatic
- Cool-headed, especially under pressure
- Aware of the situation around them and stay in control.

Great fictional examples of 'Happy High Status' are Pierce Brosnan's James Bond or Scarlett Johansson's Black Widow – both were able to kick butts, say a well-timed quip and look bloody good while doing it.

But real-life figures like Michelle Obama and the late Nelson Mandela had this power too – displaying great warmth but not losing their authority and poise. Here's how you can do it in the classroom.

How to Boost Your Authority

1) Preparation

One of the Navy Seals' mottos is: "You don't rise to the occasion but sink to the level of your training." Navy Seals (and other elite military units like the British SAS) standardise every operating procedure in the field. When they plan their missions, they look at every eventuality, roadblock and challenge that may affect the goal's success. This is so well drilled into them that they can often act without thinking and efficiently get their tasks done at lightning speed.

One thing that kills lessons and can destabilise your classrooms is when the teacher is not prepared. This is especially pertinent for early career teachers who may not have built up the experience yet. Do you know why external supply teachers and cover supervisors get a rough ride? It's because they're in an environment they don't know, teaching a subject they aren't experts in, and are unfamiliar with the school's behaviour policy to deal with problems. And boy, do the kids know this. Put your hands up if you have ever covered a lesson and a student shouted, "That's not how Sir/Ms would do it!" And it becomes a flashpoint. Yep, me too.

Make sure you prepare your lessons well and have contingencies when things go wrong. Especially if you have a rowdy class, have quick-fire activities that can get their attention or settle them down when needed. Have a seating plan and make sure that your Disruptors and Compliants are not next to each other. Have the school rules or your 'social contract' on display at all times, and act quickly and effectively when there are clear transgressions in your lessons. Having transparent systems and knowing your stuff tells your students that you have things under control, and most students will understand that the classroom is yours to run. Boss it.

2) Lower Your Reaction Time

It sounds like a tall order but trust me, there are little things that you can do to channel your inner Zen master. People with authority tend to be less reactive and ooze calm, even in the most volatile situations. Now, I am not saying we shouldn't have any emotions – if a kid verbally assaults you, I would expect you to have steam coming out of your collar. But the key is to stay in control of yourself and the situation.

The main thing you must do is to 2-5 seconds to your responses. When something significant happens, we instantly want to react and read our kids the 'Riot Act', but more often than not, responding emotionally doesn't get us the results we want – it's often the opposite.

Holocaust survivor, psychiatrist and philosopher Viktor Frankl once stated, "Between the stimulus and response, there is a space. In that space lies our freedom and power to choose our response.

In those choices lie our growth and happiness.[3]" Unless the situation is immediately life-threatening (i.e. your student is going to get hit by a bus), you don't need to react immediately. Instead, take a breath and calmly state what you want out of the situation. That breath allows you to steady your central nervous system, and your calm response will exude confidence and authority.

Salespeople often use a 'pregnant pause' where they will state their offer and immediately keep quiet to put pressure on the buyer. Whoever can stay quiet for the longest is usually in charge of the situation. Sometimes it's better to let the pause hang, as it creates tension, which forces the other person to look at their behaviour. This works absolutely brilliantly with Compliants – give it a spin!

3) Be Decisive

Mean what you say and say what you mean. Let's be honest, if you have ever worked for a leader who constantly changes their mind, gets in a muddle, and second-guesses themselves regularly, it makes you uneasy. If something needs to get done, dithering about it won't solve the problem.

The word 'decision' comes from the Latin root word 'caedere', which means 'to cut'. Making a decision often means cutting off other possibilities, which can be tricky.

Over the years, as both a teacher and a leader, I developed a framework to help me make decisions. If you have time, follow these steps.

A) Be transparent – If an important decision has to be made, tell your students or colleagues precisely what it is. Your willingness to tell the truth will help your students and team trust you and make them more likely to want to help.

B) Welcome other voices – Don't be afraid to ask for opinions. Your students or colleagues can sometimes see things from angles that you can't, and it can bring you new information that can help solve the problem.

C) Once you have made the decision, follow it through – Make your choice and push forward. The late Four-Star General and the first US African American Secretary of State Colin Powell once said, "When we are debating an issue, loyalty means giving me your honest opinion, whether you think I'll like it or not. Disagreement, at this stage, stimulates me. But once a decision has been made, the debate ends. From that point on, loyalty means executing the decision as if it were your own[4]."

Be assertive and try to follow it through. Of course, you might have to make tweaks along the way, but ensure you stay the course and give yourself time to see some results. Try not to make big decisions in the heat of the moment – one tip that has helped me make tough decisions is to give myself a day or two to step back to reflect on the situation and 'sleep on it'. It allows me to be objective and approach the problem from multiple angles. Try it!

How to Boost Your Warmth

Great leaders know how to create and use positive energy to help them lead their teams and gain support for the cause. In fact, great leaders have a lot in common with stand-up comedians – let's see why.

1) Think Like a Late Night Talk Show Host

The late-night talk show host has a tough job to do. Whether it is Graham Norton, Jonathan Ross or Lily Singh, they have to juggle their rowdy audience, difficult guests and demanding producers, all with a smile on their faces.

Kind of like being a teacher.

Great talk show hosts mix a sharp wit and assertiveness with empathy and emotional intelligence. They know how to talk to the grumpy film actor and the crazy rock star while seated on the same couch!

Talk show hosts have an amazing knack for using humour to disarm even the prickliest interviewees.

Use your humour to expose awkward truths lightly or defuse tension. In many instances, a well-placed joke can steer you away from an ugly situation brewing in the classroom. Remember, it's difficult to be angry and happy simultaneously, so use humour to lighten the drama.

I once knew a teacher who walked through the playground and tripped over in front of 500 secondary school children. Awkward.

This could have been incredibly embarrassing, but he kicked out his legs and made it into a breakdance move, turning it from embarrassment to triumph, earning the students' respect and getting fist-bumps all the way to the staffroom.

As a teacher, you need to "read the room" and understand who your learners are. So keep your humour light and breezy. If you are unsure about your humour, use the 'Line Manager Test': if your manager was in the classroom, would you be happy to say that quip? If not, then bin it.

2) Improvise Like a Stand-Up Comedian

It is said that improv comedy is the most challenging type to perform in the business. It's just you, a mic and an impatient crowd. No script, no rehearsal, no do-overs. If you don't tickle their funny bones quickly, you will bomb harder than the US military.

Great improv comedians like Amy Poehler, Jim Carrey and Jason Sudekis can 'slow time down' and become ultra-observant. In the moment, they can ask questions that allow them to bend reality for laughs.

I know that you have your lessons planned to the nanosecond, but make sure to create blocks of time where you can engage with your class and ask those 'why' questions. Set the basic parameters of what you want to teach but allow yourself to go down some rabbit holes.

Experiment a little.

Throw out left-field ideas that your class can discuss, and don't be afraid to admit that you don't know something. Allow your students to become 'classroom conspiracists' and allow them to question your lesson. If they are asking questions, they are engaging.

If you have budding comedians who may disrupt your lessons rather than battle them, get to know them better and see if they can add something to what you are teaching for future classes.

By working with their talents, not only are you stopping the disruption, but you will be building a relationship with them that will give you significant influence.

Light-hearted, friendly banter is NOT the enemy of your classrooms. The students are trying to let you in on the joke. Use this force to your advantage rather than have it used against you.

The key is to be light, open and willing to stay in the moment. If you can do this, you have won half the battle.

3) Win the Trust of Your Students like a Satirist

It has been said that 'dark times are great for comedians'. If that's the case, most comedians should be swimming in Scrooge McDuck-like pools of money after the COVID pandemic!

In uncertain times, people tend to turn to a different type of humour, called 'satire'. According to the *Cambridge Dictionary*, satire is "a way of criticising people or ideas in a humorous way, especially in order to make a political point[5]."

In the UK, shows like *Have I Got News For You* or *Mock The Week* tirelessly make fun of, parody and mock the political class and decision-makers for what they decide for the country. In the US, hosts like John Colbert, Trevor Noah, Jon Stewart and Bill Maher use politics to build their comedy routines and encourage debate about the day's hot topics.

DISENGAGEMENT/HOSTILITY

But why do the public watch comedians take down and ridicule their authorities? Shouldn't the population rally around their leaders in darker times rather than criticise them?

TV critic John Doyle wrote that the importance of satire usually occurs "at key points in history, usually when the mass of common people gets fed up with the nonsense being fed to them by politicians, political pundits, inane celebrities and the very rich[6]."

In the age where politicians, celebrities and influencers have spin-doctors on speed dial and in our post-truth media era, most people find it hard to decipher what is real. We are all so tired of being spoon-fed the same PR-sanctioned nonsense that we are forced to swallow.

A great satirist is brave enough to expose the holes, double standards, and speaks truth to power in a way many of us can't. They can be a voice to those who have felt forgotten, and can be the 'canaries in the coal mine' to point out the wrongs in our society.

Please do not get me wrong: not all satirists are 'lovely people' – some are downright destructive and vile. But they are popular because their authenticity and courage help them to win an audience who will trust what they say, especially when they know their leaders are stiffing them.

If you want your students to follow you, they have to feel that they can trust you. Period. Here are a couple of things that you can do build trust.

A) Have Integrity – Be a person of your word. If you say you will do something, make sure you follow through. Try not to lie or gaslight your students. This is perhaps the biggest trust killer in your classroom relationships if you are caught. Instead, follow-up and follow through.

B) Don't be afraid to show your principles – Don't be scared to display your personal values and the things that you stand for. Sometimes we may do or say things just to go along with the crowd, but this chips away our integrity and courage, and guess what? Having courage makes you a candidate for being a great leader.

C) Be authentic and foster trust – Don't be silly with this one. When I mean authentic, I don't mean you show the 'authenticity' that you have at 11pm on a Friday night after you have had a couple of vodkas and cranberries, but from a professional and boundaried sense, let your students into your world.

Don't be frightened to share your likes or dislikes or what you are passionate about. As you know, I'm an ardent Arsenal fan, and more often than not, it's been an extremely frustrating experience! But the conversations in my classes and tutor groups are enhanced by the banter, and it helps me peek a little bit into my students' world, which helps me connect and understand them more. As Stephen M. R. Covey wrote in *The Speed of Trust*, "contrary to what most people believe, trust is not some soft, illusive quality... rather, trust is a pragmatic, tangible, actionable asset that you can create[7]." The more trust someone has in you (and you in them), the more likely you will make positive outcomes happen. If your students trust you, they will follow your direction with little resistance. So work on building that asset.

OK, that's the end of Part 2 – pop open your notebooks and reflect.

REFLECTION QUESTIONS

1. Be honest with yourself – Do you have 'Happy High Status'? According to Viv Groskop's quote, in social situations, are you the life of the party or do you tend to fade into the background? Do you feel rejuvenated after interacting with many people or feel drained?

2. Do you feel that you are well prepared for most lessons in terms of handling behaviour? If you are, what's going well, and how can you enhance it? If you're not, can you identify what has gone wrong and how you can correct it?

3. Do you feel like you have gained the trust of the majority of your students? If you have, what methods did you use? Was it natural, or was there something you specifically did? If a student doesn't respond well to you, what do you think is the barrier, and how can you overcome it?

PRACTICAL TIPS

1. There are a lot of tools in this chapter that I have gathered to help you boost your leadership persona. Go back to the exercise you did in 'The Leadership Zone Part 1: Shadow and The Persona' and look at your classroom management style. Identify an area you want to improve on and take one of the practical tips in this chapter and practice it for a week. Look for quick wins – don't expect huge improvements straight away. My aim when I train teachers is to get them to be 1% better every day. If you continue to do that for the year, you could potentially be three times better than you are now. Practice and be patient.

2. I recognise that some people are either extroverted and introverted. Very loosely, extroverted people thrive in social situations and get stimulated around people. Introverted people enjoy solitude more and may feel drained if they interact with people for long periods. Believe it or not, I'm an introvert and find sustained interactions make me feel tired and irritable. But that doesn't mean I'm less effective – introverts rock too. You don't have to be an extrovert to be charismatic. Find a style you like and do you. As long as it helps you in your classroom, I am happy – do whatever makes you comfortable and practice self-care when needed.

3. When we think of great fictional teachers like Samuel L. Jackson's Ken Carter in *Coach Carter* or Robin Williams' John Keating in *Dead Poets Society*, they were teachers who were willing to bend (or break) the rules for their students' benefit. For any senior leaders who have just spat out their tea, relax. I'm not

suggesting that any of you do illegal things to 'serve' your kids, but I'm encouraging you to be innovative – do things a little different, stir up the pot! You have much more flexibility than you think, and you can make your classrooms exciting places rather than torture chambers. Look online for different ways to teach your students, talk to colleagues; heck, send a carrier pigeon to someone – just do something different! Your students will remember you and appreciate you for it!*

* If you want ideas on how to spice up your lessons, check out my chapter "Don't Be Boring" in AHT1. There are simple, practical ideas that you can use there. Thank me later.

THE LEADERSHIP ZONE PART 3: WHAT JÜRGEN KLOPP CAN TEACH YOU ABOUT CLASSROOM LEADERSHIP – A CASE STUDY

There are sports people.

Then there are icons.

We all know them. Let me reel off a few names to lubricate your mind:

Kobe Bryant

Usain Bolt

Muhammad Ali

Maradona

Serena Williams

Megan Rapinoe

It's not only that they are good at what they do – they wouldn't be in the conversation if they weren't masters of their craft. What separates these folks from the rest of the pack is they have the real 'X-Factor' – that je-ne-sais-quoi, that touch of genius that lifts them out of their field and puts them at the centre of our culture.

When it comes to football coaching, the man that I am going to talk about has this in spades. At this time of writing, Jürgen Norbert Klopp (born 1967) is the men's Liverpool FC's football manager. The 6-foot-4 German is known for his gregarious smile, blunt but humorous press conferences, and explosive passion on the touchlines, igniting the players and crowd alike.

Klopp came to Liverpool in the 2015-2016 season after the previous manager, Brendan Rodgers, fell desperately short of winning the Premier League. Liverpool, a club with a rich history of winning both at home and abroad, brought Klopp from Borussia Dortmund to revitalise 'The Reds' and take them back to the summit of club football.

I hope whoever hired Klopp got a bloody fat pay rise because gosh darnit, they were absolutely right.

Since Klopp has taken over Liverpool, Klopp and his 'mentality monsters' (more on that later) have snatched every single trophy that club football offers. Their trophy haul includes the Champions League title, FA Cup, UEFA Super Cup, FIFA Club World Cup, and he was the man that brought Liverpool's first-ever Premier League title in the modern era.

Before I go on, some of you might be rolling your eyes thinking, 'Why is Karl talking about football? I hate football, and it's soooooo boring.'

First of all, what is wrong with you? Everyone loves football. (Only teasing.) But more seriously, Jürgen Klopp's superpowers are how to lead people and create and sustain a culture that produces winning results. Don't you want that for your students?

Mike Gordon, the President of Fenway Sports Group (FSG), the consortium that owns Liverpool, said of Klopp, "I spent 30 years as an investor, speaking to some of the best CEOs in the world, and Jürgen is right up there with them. If he wasn't managing a football club, he could be managing a Fortune 500 company[8]." Now, that's a person that I would love to learn from. And I am sure you would too.

For the non-football fans, I will try to keep it light on the pitch-side details and look at how we can extract four lessons from the 'Boss at the Kopp' and make our classrooms world-class for our students and our schools.

Lesson 1: Create a Vision and Rally Everyone Around It

When Klopp came to Liverpool, it was a club in transition. While a very astute and professional coach, Klopp's predecessor, Brendan Rodgers, was seen as a mismatch to the direction Liverpool wanted to go in. Due to hierarchical tensions, questionable signings and an abysmal start to the season, Rodgers was dismissed.

Enter Jürgen.

The boisterous Black Forest native strolled into Anfield as cool as a cucumber. In his ebony John Wick blazer, midnight black shirt and fitted denim-blue jeans, Klopp arrived at his first press conference like a man who would take your mum to the O2 Arena to watch an ABBA reunion concert. Snazzy.

Klopp was already a respected football manager, shepherding Borussia Dortmund's youthful squad to two back-to-back

Bundesliga (The German Premier League) titles. But expectations were at fever pitch – could Klopp take them back to the top? So, naturally, the reporters peppered him with a thousand variations of this question.

Klopp pondered and replied coolly, "If I sit here in four years, I am pretty confident we will have one title." Klopp initially signed a three-year deal with an option for a one-year extension. A little later, when asked how he would manage the expectations of the Liverpool fans, who wanted Liverpool to relive the glories of the past, he stated, "Twenty-five years ago (since the last league title) is a long time. History is only the base for us, (we shouldn't) keep the history in our backpack all day[9]."

And bang on his prediction, he won the Champions League in 2019 within four years of his tenure, and did so much more.

As teachers, you must create a culture of aspiration in your classrooms. You're not merely there to help them pass exams and read texts from people that lived 400 years ago, but you're there to help your students rewrite their own personal histories. You're there to help a child break a generational cycle of poverty, substance abuse and misery through the power of education. You're there to help a student develop the self-confidence to embrace what makes them different and be able to stand up proudly in society. I know this sounds very fluffy, but it's true. Human beings have always been drawn to people who have exciting visions: whether for good, like Martin Luther King, or evil, like Attila the Hun.

But the key takeaway you must learn is that you can't do it alone. In the Information Age, we must move from being lecturers to coaches, teaching our students what they need to learn and why they need to know it.

Especially when you're with a new class, you must enter the classroom and create a culture where you work together for the common good. Find out what your students' dreams are and tie your lessons to them. If you succeed, your students will be more responsive and willing to hear what you say. Remember, if you show interest in them, they will show interest in you.

Lesson 2: Have a Clear Structure and Make Sure Everyone Understands Their Role

Klopp is lauded not only for his charisma but his ability to boil down complex game strategies into very simple philosophies and get his players to 'buy in' to them. Klopp is surrounded by a galaxy of stars with insane talent, but he also recognises that each member must play their part so that the whole team can win.

His most significant change was implementing what he called 'heavy metal football'. This style of play pressurised Liverpool's opponents into making a mistake high up the pitch, and then, in the blink of an eye, The Reds would regain possession and score a goal without even giving the rival players the time to blink[10].

Klopp doesn't accept any passengers on his team. Liverpool hunt, harass and dominate their opponents. If their opponents try their strategy, Liverpool will win the ball and hit them on the counter. Few teams can go toe-to-toe with Liverpool because of this aggressive football philosophy.

DISENGAGEMENT/HOSTILITY

Look, I'm not suggesting you participate in 'heavy metal teaching'. I don't want you to hunt, harass and dominate your students – you will lose your job. But what is critically important is that you ensure everyone explicitly understands their roles in the classroom and create an atmosphere where everyone can succeed. There need to be clear lines for rewards and clear lines for sanctions. Ambiguity is the father of poor behaviour management. You must create consistent structures and expectations, including how your students enter the room, the classroom routines, and the homework submission quality. Hone these practices until your classes know it like the back of their hands, and you will have a much smoother lesson.

Lesson 3: Intentionally Build Trust and Rapport in Your Classrooms

Before Klopp signs a player, he seeks an opportunity to have a one-to-one meeting with the individual to find out what makes them 'tick'. He will ask about their family and their interests in and out of their football career. The reasoning is simple: the fact that the player is in his office shows he is extremely good at football. Klopp wants a deeper understanding of the player's mentality to assess what the person is like, whether they will fit into the team, and how he can support and help that player improve.

Pepijn Lijnders, the current Assistant Manager of Liverpool, stated, "Jürgen creates a family. We always say: 30 per cent tactics, 70 per cent teambuilding[11]." Klopp instinctively understands that any team with the right players, a lack of injuries, and a little luck can do well in the Premier League. But to build sustained success like Liverpool over many years, you must ensure that you can retain players, motivate them and keep them on task as the seasons wear on.

Klopp nicknamed his players "mentality monsters" because of their ability to be resilient and give everything on the pitch, often snatching victory from the jaws of defeat. However, the only way to truly maintain these standards is if trust, rapport and warmth are nurtured in the team.

Let's be honest: as modern teachers, our jobs are to help our students get the grades they need. For many of our students (especially in secondary education), this can feel like a daunting task – five years of study boiling down to a month of exams during the Summer Term. But like Klopp, you can maintain a culture where you are not only looking at their academic needs but their emotional and mental ones, and you will help them develop the resilience and fortitude that will increase their chances of success.

Create spaces where the students can talk about their worries or concerns. Plan activities where they can blow off steam and have a little fun once in a while. Ask genuine questions about their welfare. If you do that successfully, you will find that your students will start going the extra mile for you and themselves because they have the emotional security and reassurance that you have their back.

Lesson 4: Enforce Discipline and Demand High Standards

But don't get it twisted. Behind the charisma, the smiles and the amusing press conferences is a steely tactician who demands the

DISENGAGEMENT/HOSTILITY

highest standards from his players. The players know who the Boss is, and they know not to cross Klopp.

When it is time to work, the players must be 100% switched on and ready to go. In a *Guardian* report that chronicled Liverpool's first modern Premier League title, the reporter, Andy Hunter, picked up on Klopp's fastidious and sometimes relentless nature. Hunter stated, "To Klopp, the training ground is sacred. Respecting Melwood as a place of work is his absolute rule. There is no leeway on that instruction, a point he enforced by banning impromptu visits from wives and partners, agents and hangers-on as soon as he arrived." The Croatia international Dejan Lovren, who worked with Klopp in 2015, once quipped, "He's your friend but he's not your best friend[12]."

Being kind yet demanding is not a contradiction. Our students are human and will cross the lines, no matter how empathetic you are. Tempers will get heated, words will be said, standards will be dropped, and you must be ready and willing to uphold your high-performance culture.

In my first book, in the chapter "How To Sanction Effectively", I went through a step-by-step process of how to give sanctions without feeling like a dictator. But to summarise my points, you must get your approach right. 'Punishment' is very different from 'discipline'. Punishing people is about retribution, and it comes from a darker place. When we punish people, we want to inflict pain on them, and in the moment, we do not care about whether it is for their betterment. 'Discipline' is a different animal. It's less emotional and more surgical. This is about correcting the poor behaviour, so they can have a better future outcome and grow more mature.

When you sanction your students for infractions, ensure that the sanctions are just, proportionate and effective. Sanctions that drag on are just as bad as no sanctions at all. Once it is done and your student has learned their lesson, give them grace and swiftly move on from the incident. If you can do that well, it will demonstrate practical and decisive leadership.

REFLECTION QUESTIONS

1. Are you a team player or prefer to work solo? Have you tried to establish working relationships with your colleagues? If so, how well are they working and can you improve them? If not, what is holding you back?

2. I want you to think of someone you admire as a leader. Ideally, this would be someone you know personally in education, but if not, it could be in another sector or even a celebrity like Jürgen Klopp. What is it about them that you admire? What does that person do that other leaders don't?

3. If you are teaching, I want you to reflect on the best class you currently teach and the worst class you deal with. What are the factors that make your best and worst classes different? (Please don't just say the kids – look deeper, young grasshopper.) How do you 'show up' in these classes? Are they the same, or are they different? Why?

PRACTICAL TIPS

1. To be great at classroom management, you must learn how to work as part of a unit. As great as Klopp is, he would have never been able to do it on his own. Everyone from the canteen staff to Liverpool's owners has a part to play in the team's success on and off the pitch. Make sure that you network effectively in your organisation. Learn who the Heads of Department are, the curriculum specialists, Heads of Years, etc. Have a chat, and when you have established that rapport, pick their brains on students and teaching practice – your colleagues are an absolute goldmine of resources and assistance. Of course, ensure that you're adding value to them and helping them out. Don't be a parasite. If you are in a good school, everyone will come together to get the best possible outcomes for the students you teach. If not, then you need to leave. Also, go beyond your physical school. Use social media to enhance your practice. Platforms like LinkedIn and Twitter have thriving communities of dedicated teachers who want to help each other succeed and share best practices. Much of the success of *The Action Hero Teacher* came from my online networks. The teaching world is small and, you never know; you could become an 'edu-influencer' based on what you share – try it!*

2. As I mentioned in the chapter "Teaching Generation Z", we live in a time of extreme disruption and crisis. At this time of writing, because of the ongoing conflicts in Eastern Europe, the tectonic plates of the global hierarchy are shifting, and it is becoming harder to predict what will happen in five months, let alone five

years. One of the hallmarks of a transitioning society is extreme distrust of the institutions that govern it, and yes, this includes education. More than ever, our Generation Z students will question, critique and sometimes disregard what we have to say. Because of the explosive growth of social media, our students are used to having their voices heard and acknowledged. That's why the days of 'teaching by force' is limited. Learning how to coach as well as lecture is imperative to teachers today. As teachers, we are brilliant at explaining the 'how' of our subject but not the 'why'. This generation is more entrepreneurial and self-sufficient than ever, so we need to key into their intrinsic motivations to do things**.

3. Many teachers struggle with disciplining/sanctioning their students. It's natural – especially in the beginning – because a sanction acknowledges something has gone wrong. But I want you to remember these key points. A) You sanction not to inflict pain but course correct. This is for the long-term welfare of the student. B) You must, must, must have the Ground Rules clearly displayed in your classroom. At the beginning of the year or when you start with your new class, spend some time and go through each rule – there should be no room for confusion. Then, when they make an error, refer to the rules and clarify what they have done wrong and how they can correct it.

4. If the student does not adequately correct their error, follow through with your procedures. If you or the student are 'emotionally hijacked', don't be afraid to send the child elsewhere (to the corridor, to another class) or walk away from the situation. Once it has calmed down, inform them of the consequence and

follow through. But once they have done their sanction and are sincere in their apology, please move on. If you continue to bring up the past, you risk destroying the relationship and increasing the likelihood of future flashpoints. As the students would say, 'Make sure you squash the beef.***'

* For practical tips on how to build a team in your school, refer to the AHT1 chapter, "Assemble Your Team".

** I have a great chapter in AHT1 called "Casting A Vision", which will give you a step-by-step guide to tap into your students' dreams and aspirations and use that to help keep them motivated and engaged – have a look!

*** For more help in ground rule setting in AHT1, check out the section "The Rules vs The Social Contract".

MEET 'THE DISRUPTORS' – THE SIX TYPES OF CHARACTERS THAT WILL RUIN YOUR LESSONS AND HOW TO DEAL WITH THEM

Using my 'Trust Mountain' theory, right at the bottom of the pyramid are the lovely students known as Disruptors. These individuals are the types who make your teaching career an absolute crap show. Nine out of ten flashpoint situations start with aggression, and in the words of Doctor Strange, "Things can get out of hand."

But since writing the original book, conducting training sessions, talking to other teachers and reflecting on my practice, I realised that these lovely students come in their own distinct flavours and will need slightly different treatments.

This chapter is designed to give you a whistle-stop tour of what types of behaviour you should expect from our disruptive students and some quick tactics to help you manage the situation like a classroom management pro. In the words of Batman, "Action is what is called for. Talking is for the birds[13]", and you will get it here!

Remember, some of these behaviours may overlap, but trying something quickly is better than having a face full of chair.

There tend to be two types of hostility you face in the classroom, labelled simply as overt and covert aggression.

Overt Aggression

We all know what outright aggression looks like... and that should never be tolerated.

But some clever aggressors use creative tactics to keep us in a loop. Let's look at some strategies in their playbook and how to nullify them effectively. This may seem elementary, but I've consulted enough teachers to know this is surprisingly common.

Mike Tyson once said that people get knocked out by the punches they don't see, and I hope these descriptions will give you the catlike reflexes to dodge and counter hostility easily.

Here are three types of overt aggressors.

1. Habitual Line Steppers

In the legendary comedy series, *The Chapelle Show*, the late, great Charlie Murphy recounted hilarious stories about his misadventures with his younger brother Eddie in the 1980's celebrity scene.

In the '80s, Eddie Murphy was one of the biggest stars in Hollywood, known for his movies and comedy specials. Charlie, an ex-Navy officer, acted as Eddie's security, often putting a swift and brutal end to any attempts to disturb his brother.

But Charlie met his match in funk singer and mischief-maker, the late Rick James. As the story goes, Rick James was mercurial;

alternating between friendly, cheerful banter with Charlie to physically assaulting him, usually by slamming his face into tables and throwing drinks at him. Charlie hilariously coined the term 'habitual line stepper' to describe James' behaviour and his frustrations in dealing with him.

I don't expect your students to slam your head into furniture, but Murphy's quote perfectly describes this type of aggressor. Habitual line steppers (HLSs) tend to invade your physical space and use their body as a tool to intimidate you.

Even if their facial expressions are friendly, HLSs will display threatening body language, especially if these individuals happen to be taller or more muscular than you. They may not only invade your space but grab items that are associated with you as an act of dominance. Think of an old-school gangster movie like *Goodfellas*, where the Mafiosos shake down local businesses to make them pay 'protection money', then you get the idea.

How to Deal with Habitual Line Steppers

This is very simple: call out their behaviour, calmly but firmly. This is a battle of territory. The more space that you give up, the more emboldened they become. The mistake most teachers make is, because of the shock and fear of dealing with an HLS, they give in to their intimidation until they are stuck like Baby in the corner from *Dirty Dancing*. But no one like Patrick Swayze can save you.

In a calm but firm tone, call out their behaviour, spelling out precisely what they are doing and what you want them to do next. For example:

"Ben, you are now invading my personal space, and it seems like you are trying to intimidate me. So I am politely asking you to take a few steps back and we will discuss what happens next."

Never, ever, ever accept someone invading your personal space. If this is a persistent occurrence, you must flag it up through the proper channels. It's totally unacceptable. Protect your personal space at all costs.

2. Pressurisers

Whereas 'Habitual Line Steppers' use their bodies to intimidate you, pressurisers use their words to get you under control. Unfortunately, this classic bully tactic is very popular with troublesome students (and awful managers).

A pressuriser's world is very 'black-and-white'. Pressurisers cannot tolerate nuance, don't believe in concepts like negotiation or compromise, and love to give out ultimatums – with both options putting you at a disadvantage.

Pressurisers raise their voices and give you ultimatums with little time to think it over. They instinctually know the person who calls the shots tends to be the one in charge, and this stance allows them to control the 'frame' of the conversation. The more you try to resist, the angrier and more belligerent they become. Like a boa constrictor, this behaviour is designed to tighten their hold over you until you give in.

How to Deal with Pressurisers

The psychology of the pressuriser is simple: they know that most people don't like confrontation, and they know that tense situations knock people emotionally 'off-kilter'. Have you ever had a time where, out of the blue, you received some terrifying news? For example, imagine you received a call where a loved one has fallen extremely ill and has even been rushed to the hospital. How would you feel? Overwhelmed? Shaken? Numb? This is precisely what pressurisers want to induce in you, as you will not be in the best frame to make good decisions.

The first step is to slow things down and take a deep breath. At this point, your nervous system is lighting up like a Christmas tree. Your breath helps to stop you from entering an 'emotional hijacking'. Even counting down three seconds in your head before you reply helps: it takes the focus away from the aggressor and back onto you.

Talk slowly, calmly and firmly, reasserting your boundaries. Don't automatically give in to the pressuriser's ultimatum. This approach shows them that you are not taking the bait, and they can't provoke you into a firefight. Always remember, the calmest person in the room wins. If they continue to push on with this behaviour, use your standard sanctioning protocols or call for help.

The sad fact is that aggressors will choose their victims on the perceived ease of dominance. Most of the time, these types target someone they believe won't give them much trouble.

Although it is daunting, standing up for yourself (professionally and politely) will show the aggressor that you are not 'easy' and gradually, they will learn to respect you. On the other hand, if you don't stand up for yourself, this will encourage their behaviour, and they become even more aggressive towards you.

Boundaries are your friend – use them!

3. The Insult Comics

We all know them: Jimmy Carr, Frankie Boyle, Paul Chowdhry, Amy Schumer, Chris Rock, Jamie Foxx. These comedians are a heckler's worst nightmare. They use their words like ancient samurai masters used their katanas, ruthlessly cutting down anyone unfortunate enough to cross them (especially if you sit at the front of a comedy show – NEVER, EVER sit at the front of a comedy show). Unfortunately, we sometimes have these guys sitting in our class, ready to cut us down to size.

These students will use cutting humour towards you, claiming it's 'banter'. There is nothing wrong with a bit of humour but their jokes are designed to demean, belittle or discredit their intended target. An insult comic's statements are usually dripping with contempt – followed by a smirk when they know they have irked their target. Whoever said "Sticks and stones may break my bones, but words will never hurt me" is a flipping liar and needs the 'back-of-the-shed-treatment'.

When you reinforce your boundaries with these insult comics, they will 'reverse-uno' you and leverage the situation to make you look like you are picking on them. For example, if you regularly hear phrases like:

> "What did I do?"
> "What's your problem?"

DISENGAGEMENT/HOSTILITY

"Can't you take a joke?"
"What's wrong with this teacher? Oh, my dayyyyys!"
"You're being way too sensitive."

... this is insult comic territory. Especially when you are meeting a class for the time, you may find yourself in this situation, and even the HLS or the pressurisers may use this to test the waters and test your mettle. Remember, these students are trying to get a 'rise' out of you – if you react emotionally, they have succeeded in getting under your skin.

How to Deal with Insult Comics

There are two ways you can approach this.

1) The 'Sweet' Approach. If a student is pushing the envelope and you're not sure whether they are making a dig at you, try this: after the insulting comment, take a breath, smile and simply say:

"That's really funny! It did sound a little insulting, but I'm going to assume it's a little joke – it would be a *shame* to kill the positive vibe in the class." (It also helps to say it with a bit of sarcasm so they can pick up that you are not pleased.)

If they're sensible, they will backtrack and apologise. Say this politely yet firmly. That clearly conveys that it's not OK, and you're giving the insult comic a warning shot.

2) The 'Sour' Approach. If they continue or say something particularly insulting, again, in a polite yet firm voice say, "That's not funny, and you have crossed the line. Don't do that again."

Eight times out of ten, these approaches should shut down the insult comics. If not, just follow your sanctioning procedures. In the first book, I spoke about creating a 'Social Contract' – a set of mutually-agreed rules designed to increase the 'buy-in' from your students and minimise flashpoint situations.

In my experience, insult comics can kill a classroom's camaraderie and emotional safety. If people do not feel safe, they can often react unpredictably. At the 2022 Oscars, the altercation between Will Smith and Chris Rock showed us how one joke can lead to a very violent and shocking outcome. So don't allow it to fester in your classrooms.

In summary, you must lay down your boundaries with overtly aggressive types, so they don't see you as a 'pushover'. Once they see they are not getting their way, aggressors will sooner or later back down and identify an easier target.

Covert Aggression

This type is harder to spot (well duh, obviously).

Covert aggression is also known as 'passive aggression.' Covert aggressors don't like outright confrontation but will indirectly make life harder for you and others.

When I played *Call of Duty*, a popular Battle Royale-style war game, with my nephew many years ago, when we landed on the map, my nephew would find the nearest sniper rifle and plant himself on the highest vantage point. He would then proceed to terrorise me, sniping me from a distance, and I felt there was no way to fight back.

Covert aggressors also work like this, finding unique angles to disrupt the class and sometimes you are none the wiser. They could be incredibly polite and friendly, and you may even have a good relationship with them! But watch out – they can be just as disruptive as the overt types. Here are three flavours of covert disruption.

1. The Standard Droppers

Watch out for people who chronically drop the required standards that you set up in your classrooms. These guys may not be outwardly hostile, aggressive or malicious, but buck the rules. They can often be late, not wearing the correct uniform, and baulk at any rules imposed on them.

They never heed warnings and continue their behaviour, so you feel you are constantly nagging them. In my experience, the standard droppers may be hell-raisers in other classes, but because they have a little respect for you, they smooth some of their edges and will at least comply with some of your instructions. But on the other hand, they may feel that they have to live up to their reputation and not go along with your plans to show the others 'they still have it', disrupting the class when they feel like it.

All of us make mistakes and drop our standards from time to time. Of course, no one expects any of our students to be perfect. But chronic standard droppers by their behaviour show that your authority is unimportant, and will get very defensive when you ask them to align with the rest of the class.

This also undermines your authority when you try to deal with other students, as they will see you let off the repeat offender. Unfortunately, this affects the culture over time and negatively hinders your classroom management abilities.

How to Deal with Standard Droppers

You must win your students' hearts and minds, and ensure they internalise why the standards are as vital to them as they are to you. This is where mentoring becomes absolutely critical when dealing with these pupils.

If standard droppers comply with some of your instructions, the good news is they are willing to follow your lead but may need an extra push.

The first thing you must do is form a 'Social Contract' – these are a set of values that you design with your class that everyone (including you) must uphold. What makes it effective is that it gives your students ownership of their behaviour as they feel like they are a part of the process.

If you have done that right, you will have given your student ample intrinsic motivation to follow your lead. If there are still issues after you have set this up, have a heart-to-heart with them, preferably in a private space. If you try to shame them in front of their peers, this could quickly turn into a flashpoint situation.

Be curious and try to investigate why they are not following these instructions. This doesn't have to be in class, but this could be at the end of the lesson. A barrier might stop them, such as a lack of money to purchase the correct uniform, and maybe they are too embarrassed to say. See if you can get to the heart of the matter and be willing to listen.

Sadly, if all the conversations and mentoring attempts fail, you must start applying sanctions to their behaviour. They have to meet you halfway. Although this is not what any teacher wants to do, we must ensure that our rules apply to everyone. Playing favourites risks losing the rapport we have worked so hard to build with our other students.

2. The Classroom Instigators

If you have been teaching long enough, you will experience this scenario: You have a class that you run fairly well – everyone gets along, and the vibe is positive. Then your Head of Department requests that you take a particular student into your classroom. In a short time, the friendly vibe that used to permeate the room has suddenly changed:

- Students bicker more.
- People make more cutting remarks.
- Factions are created, making group work more difficult.

You can't quite put your finger on it, but you know something is amiss. Different students start approaching you after class to gossip and tittle-tattle on other members. Sometimes this escalates to verbal threats and even physical violence.

If this happens, your class may have fell victim to an instigator. Instigators are felt but not seen, and their negative influence destabilises your classrooms. This can also be seen in your workplace with adults. So beware: in an office setting, an instigator can make your work environment unbearable, and I would advise you to get HR involved or find another job. Here are a few tell-tale signs:

- Instigators are often at the centre of dramas, even though they say that they are the victims – instigators are never far away from the dramas they create and will usually whine when their names are brought into the conflict. Some clever instigators will use 'triangulation' to slander their target to other people, which will ruin their target's reputation and socially isolate them. This is even more sinister when social media is used – an instigator can set up an anonymous dummy account and destroy their target online, while pretending to be their friend in real life. This is wicked but is sadly becoming increasingly common.
- Instigators tend to fall in and out of different 'cliques', often leaving those friendship groups in disarray. Be watchful for students who jump from social circle to social circle, especially if there is always a dramatic 'breakup' where the instigator cuts everyone off and then claims their new clique are their 'BFFs'. If this happens often, it's a huge red flag.
- Instigators constantly gossip and revel in other people's misfortune. We're human; we all love a little bit of gossip. But whereas most people look at the headlines of what is happening in the day, an instigator is a 24-hour news channel, breaking the latest stories. Instigators usually have 'dirt' on everyone and are not afraid to use it. Also,

watch out for a lack of self-reflection and self-depreciation: instigators are often self-righteous, quick to point at other people's flaws, but never too quick to accept responsibility for their own mistakes.

How to Deal with Classroom Instigators

No one expects children (or adults) to get along all the time... We're all flawed beings.

But the difference is how conflict is handled. Most sensible children (and adults) do not like disharmony and will try their best to resolve lingering disputes effectively.

Unfortunately, instigators use their strategies to help them control others and hold power in their classrooms and social circles. If you look at it from a deeper psychological level, these strategies come from deep-seated insecurities. Deep down, instigators believe that people may not like them for who they are, so they find it easier to destroy others than work on bettering themselves. Unfortunately, in the brutal social jungle of school (and work), some students (and other adults) feel that is the only way to survive.

Although the threats may not be physical, the mental, emotional and psychological damage these guys can inflict can be immense and take several years to repair. Also, from my experience, the formation of cliques and hostile classroom atmospheres can lead to bullying and even physical fights if they aren't handled correctly.

Bar there are any mitigating circumstances, if you get wind of instigations in your classroom, you need to deal with them immediately. Please do not hesitate to involve your pastoral teams (Year Team, SAFE workers, counsellors).

If you get wind of any disturbances and the same names keep getting mentioned, please take heed. In the infamous book, *The 48 Laws of Power*, Robert Greene warns his readers to be wary of these negative types of people. He writes, "The incurably unhappy and unstable have a particularly strong infectious power because their characters and emotions are so intense. They present themselves as victims, making it difficult… to see their miseries as self-inflicted[14]."

Also, keep a watchful eye on the quieter members of your classroom. Sadly, the soft, timid types often get targeted for bullying by instigators and may not come forward out of fear and shame. It's essential to build relationships with students so that you can tell when something is 'off' about your pupil.

Make sure you thoroughly investigate what has been occurring in your classrooms. Speak to the individuals involved, and try to get to the bottom of any conflicts.

If possible, try to do activities that reinforce your classroom values, like harmony, cooperation and kindness.

Don't let instigators sit together in your classroom – separate them out and make it explicit why it's happening.

Keep your pastoral teams, parents and other relevant staff in the loop, especially if suspected bullying is involved.

3. Chronic Doubters

These are really tricky people to deal with...

These students (and adults) consistently question, probe and critique any decisions you make. If there is a problem, they tend only to talk about the negative aspects and never offer any constructive solutions. They tend to be highly pessimistic and the leader of any disagreements in the classroom (and workplace). They cannot accept criticism when they are wrong and often pass the blame to others. They are often resistant to change and condescending in their remarks. They cast themselves as eternal victims and usually are very thin-skinned, taking any form of criticism as a personal attack.

How to Deal with Chronic Doubters

There is a difference between 'constructive criticism' and being vindictive.

These types of aggressors say these statements to make you doubt yourself and your abilities. This starts a vicious cycle where you become more nervous around them and more prone to making mistakes they pounce on. Don't enter that cycle.

Use this strategy: ask the chronic doubter for every negative suggestion they make to come up with three positive solutions that you can discuss after the lesson (or meeting). Otherwise, unless it's a glaring mistake, ask them not to constantly interrupt your class.

Reaffirm your 'social contract', especially around kindness and respect – and if they refuse to do that, sanction as required.

REFLECTION QUESTIONS

1. If you are already teaching, think about a challenging class that you have to teach – does it contain any of the six types of Disruptors? If so, how many are there in this particular class? Have they always been in your class or moved there recently?

2. When you deal with an overt disruptor, how do you feel in your body at that particular moment? Do you feel confident and assured? Or do you feel anxious and timid? Do you think you can handle the situation, or do you feel you can't cope?

3. If you have covert disruptors in your class, how did you spot them? Do you feel like you're often being drawn into webs of intrigue and deception? And if so, how have you diffused the situation in the past?

PRACTICAL TIPS

1. First of all, let me say this off the bat. Feeling anxious and afraid is normal in the face of an aggressor. In many developed nations, using force or the threat of violence is rightly shunned, looked down upon and deterred robustly. Unfortunately, that is also why aggressive people do it – because most of us are unprepared for confrontation. The most important thing is to show calmness in the face of aggression. Most bullies and aggressors, by their nature, are insecure people. They rely upon external reactions to validate their gnawing self-doubt and anxiety. If a bully believes that they are getting their way, unfortunately, in many cases, this will embolden their actions. On the other hand, if you stand firm and are assertive and calm, you can better assess the situation and shut the flashpoint down. Also, in some cases, this may deter the aggressor because they see that what they are doing is not working and may have to change strategy. A friend once told me, 'If you are angry on the outside, be calm on the inside. If you are angry on the inside, be calm on the outside.' Have an element of calmness about you.

2. Another great tip is to channel the aggressive person's energy into something productive and pro-social. Some humans are naturally more aggressive than others – that's life. But if you have the scope, try to create tasks that allow them to show this side of themselves without causing too much disruption. Competitions, debates and quizzes are great ways to convert aggressive energy into healthy competition. It also serves the aggressor as they get the validation they want without wrecking your class.*

3. Prevention is better than a cure. Some flashpoint situations are like storms; some can come quickly without warning, or others appear like ominous storm clouds on the horizon. If your students bring you any rumours or gossip about any situations that may go down, listen and, if possible, try to deal with it yourself or flag it up to the relevant pastoral teams. Some beefs can get squashed with a short pastoral meeting, common sense and a handshake. Try to be proactive rather than reactive.**

* For more classroom tips on how to make your lessons more exciting, check out the chapter "Don't Be Boring" in AHT1.

** Check out the chapter "How To Handle A Flashpoint" for more information.

AUDIENCE

AUDIENCE INTRODUCTION

During the COVID-19 pandemic, many of our favourite sporting events were played without audiences. Football matches, racecourses and even the Olympics were played in empty stadiums. They felt barren, sterile and less fun. The shouts of delight, the gasps of agony and the bawdy chants were lost in the chaos of SARS-COV-19, and we were lesser for it.

Human energy can change the dynamic of any situation rapidly.

Chances are, many flashpoint situations that you face will involve an audience. The 'audience' is the oxygen of our flashpoints – how your audience interacts with the developing situation can turn a minor disruption into a full-blown firefight. You must learn to tame and harness audience energy to diffuse and ease the problem.

Firstly, you will learn the basic principles of group dynamics and why we behave differently in groups than when alone. Secondly, you will learn how to have difficult conversations with our social media-minded young people and how to stop your classroom from resembling a Twitter pile-on. Next, you will learn how to be an effective coach and help to guide your young people into making better decisions. And finally, you will learn how to be a good giver and get much more in return.

Let's go, champ!

GROUP DYNAMICS 101: IF YOU DON'T CONTROL THE CROWD, THE CROWD WILL CONTROL YOU

Have you ever been in a gang?

When I said 'gang', I bet you my Friday night Nando's money that you pictured sawn-off shotguns, balaclavas and East London geezers talking about "bein' 'ard" and "takin' your blinking kneecaps orf". (Clearly, I've been watching too much *Lock, Stock and Two Smoking Barrels* – great film.)

Most of you are not criminally-minded, so let me stretch the definition... When you were younger, did you hang around a group of people who got up to some 'naughty things'? I know everyone's definition of 'naughty' is completely different, but let me give you some examples to help jog your memories...

Have you ever:

- Gone on a wild holiday with your mates and got up to some things you wouldn't dare say to your loved ones?
- Secretly gone to a place with your pals that your parents didn't know about, and you lied about where you were?
- Been with your friends and said or did outrageous things that you wouldn't do alone?
- Dressed up or acted in ways you might not have wanted to, but you did it to fit in with your mates?

- Engaged in reckless behaviour with your friends, only to regret it later?

Now we're talking. I am 99.9% sure that you have done something similar to one of these things. To the 0.1% who are reading this and vehemently disagree with the above, you are either:

1) A reincarnated saint.
2) A big, fat liar.

I'll leave it there. Human beings are social animals. Our ability to come together over hundreds of thousands of years has made us the dominant species on the planet. Humans, when we come together, can do incredible things that benefit us all, such as the Suffragette and Civil Rights Movements. Also, humans in groups can do breathtakingly stupid things that are incredibly destructive, like the England fans that trashed Wembley Stadium during the Euros 2020 Final between England and Italy.

What is going on with us?

If you haven't guessed it, you are in charge of a group of students, and more often than not, they have more in common with each other than with you. This means that they often form a 'group', and if you don't manage it right, it could lead to your downfall. Therefore, dealing with 'group dynamics' is just as important as dealing with individual characters. In this chapter, you will learn the roots of our 'social behaviour' and the essential tools to influence a crowd in a way that would make the most cynical politician get emotional.

Why Chimpanzees Can't Organise the Glastonbury Festival

Chimpanzees are our closest biological 'cousins'. They can cooperate but nowhere near our level. Chimps will hang around with other chimps who are their kin or close friends, but anyone outside of their 'troop' will be engaged with hostility, regardless of what they could offer the group.

Our early ancestors were different and realised the benefits of learning to work together and cooperate, even with strangers, which may have kick-started our journey to becoming modern humans. Evolutionary social psychologist Professor William Von Hippel highlights the 'Social Brian Hypothesis' as one of the reasons we were able to separate ourselves so drastically from other primates. He writes, "[The Social Hypothesis]... is the idea that primates evolved large brains to manage social challenges inherent in dealing with other members of highly interdependent groups... Once our ancestors began reaping the benefits of teamwork, they laid the groundwork for all types of social innovations.[1]"

These social innovations included agriculture and laws, which supercharged our technological progress to modern society. Our early ancestors realised that if they helped each other, everyone could benefit from the deal. For most of us, collective action is hard-wired into our DNA, and that's why you will never see chimps organise a banging festival that features Oasis and Jay-Z on the same stage.

Why Emotions Rule Crowds

Scientists and researchers estimate that Homo sapiens appeared roughly around 300,000 years ago. These scientists also reckon that human language evolved 50,000-150,000 years ago. Even if we are kind and take the longer estimate (150,000 years), as human beings, we spent half the time without a modal language to communicate.

Humans had to evolve to accurately read and respond to body language and decipher other people's emotions. Our early human ancestors had to quickly determine who was friend or foe, who would cooperate with them, and who were the best people to reproduce with. Hundreds of thousands of years ago, there were no cops or justice system, and it was perilous when you were a hunter-gatherer. Even if you looked and fought like Dwayne 'The Rock' Johnson, if you upset enough people, when you went to sleep that night, you might end up with someone bashing in your skull with a club and making sure you have 'nap time' forever. You had to have absolute certainty that Bob and Margaret from the cave next-door weren't planning to murder you.

To do this accurately, we learned to develop social emotions like camaraderie, pride, guilt and shame to keep ourselves in tune with the group and ensure we didn't step out of line. People who were seen as liabilities to the collective were often ostracised or thrown out of the clan – which in those times usually meant certain death from the harsh terrain, starvation, wild animals or even enemy tribes. This is where we get our Fear of Missing Out (FOMO) from, and this is especially important to young people who live their lives through social media. Most of the time, appearing to have the same feelings as everyone else ensures you stay 'in' rather than get moved out.

The early humans who were more adept at learning how to do this successfully passed their genes on, and we are their successors.

What Makes Groups Tick?

Something special happens when humans come together for a common cause. Think of the last time you went to a mass event of similar-minded people. It could have been a concert to see your favourite band, a sporting event to cheer on your favourite team, or even going to a place of worship and being connected to other worshippers. How did you feel?

For most of us, when we feel that synergy with others, jacks up our 'feel-good' hormones like serotonin and dopamine, and it can feel like a transcendent experience. But sadly, this can be used for evil intent – if you look at the rallies that Adolf Hitler conducted in the run-up to World War II, he managed to whip up his followers into a frenzy and plunge our world into darkness.

When we are in the thralls of this 'group force', we may do things that we wouldn't dream of doing on our own and outside of its influence, we regret later. That's why reflecting on your decisions is essential away from the madding crowd.

In his brilliant book, *The Laws of Human Nature*, author and strategist Robert Greene identifies four elements that glue groups together and keep them in harmony[2].

1) The desire to fit in – There is nothing more addictive than feeling like you belong in a group.

2) The need to perform – We feel that we must conform to show others that we belong to the group. We tend to downplay our flaws and exaggerate our strengths.

3) Emotional contagion – We tend to pick up and copy the emotions of others in the group

4) Hypercertainty – Being in a group makes us feel braver, more confident and more willing to act, and can also mean that we are more willing to take risks.

This will explain your teenage delinquent exploits – yes, I am also talking to you, you so-called saints. Here's the rub, folks: leadership is tough. As a teacher, you are in a position of leadership. If the group (i.e. the class that you teach) doesn't believe that what you're doing serves their best interests, they may comply with the rules you set but will undermine you at the nearest opportunity.

It is not enough just to show up, blast your title and expect your students to listen to you. That's the 'old-school' way of handling behaviour. You can't just win their attention – you must win their hearts and minds.

If you are not aware of how group dynamics affect your classes, you will never be able to truly engage your students. In an age where students can tweet at prime ministers and presidents and tell them and their mums where to go, it is naive to think that our titles protect us. We have to adapt.

And here's how.

1) Make Your Class Inclusive

Make your class welcoming and inviting, and make your students want to come to your lessons. Make it clear from the beginning that they can contribute and make their voices heard if they respect everyone in the room. This is critical if you teach students not from the same social, racial, religious, gender or economic context as you.

Talking from experience, students who are not very well-represented in society are often marginalised and looked over, creating many barriers to their learning. Well-meaning yet misinformed educators may worsen the situation by their behaviour and what they say. Make sure you get to know your students, understand their origins, and respect who they are. Ask questions and be curious – try to step into your students' shoes and understand their unique points of view.

2) Spread Positive Vibes

You are the emotional bellwether of your classroom. Emotions, as we have already established, are contagious. We cannot overnight undo hundreds of thousands or possibly millions of years of genetic programming. Your students (even the naughty ones) are constantly scanning your face and body movements to get clues about your state of mind, taking their cues from there.

Don't believe me? Try this experiment: pick any class you teach, and when they enter the room, have a neutral face, be as silent as possible and stare blankly at them without talking. Notice how they respond to you. Some will be puzzled, and some will ask you if you are OK and might be genuinely concerned about your welfare. Some will start looking around nervously - this is all from the power of body language and silence. In the chapter "Pattern Interrupts", we established that you could use this type of odd behaviour to your advantage. Your body is a valuable communication tool.

Practice having 'Happy High Status', and the class will follow your example. Refer to the earlier chapter.

3) Have a Seating Plan

This is obvious, but it goes without saying. Most Disruptors feed off audience participation and will be encouraged if they have like-minded individuals sitting near them. If they are not following your lead, their disruptive behaviour can be an emotional contagion in your class. Once a group of Disruptors are together, their disruptive power doesn't add – it multiplies. One of the simplest ways to stop this is to make sure the stronger characters don't get the opportunity to distract you and others in the lesson. A seating plan is your best friend.

REFLECTION QUESTIONS

1. Think of a time when you were in a group session with strangers. How did the people generally behave? Who became the 'leaders' of the group? What did they do to display dominance?

2. Think of one of your challenging classes. Who are the 'Disruptors' in the room? How do they affect the behaviour of the students around them? Which students are more susceptible to being influenced by Disruptors? What is the classroom like when the Disruptors are away?

3. In general, what mood do you establish in the classroom? Are you a happy, upbeat teacher, or do you prefer to be stoic and strict? Have you tried to create a different 'vibe' in the classroom? How did that go?

PRACTICAL TIPS

1. If you are an educator who teaches children from a different context, please do NOT pretend that you don't see their differences. This is the fastest way to turn these young people against you. Learn how to pronounce your students' names and get them right every time. If your students are using words you are unfamiliar with, as long as they are respectful, be curious and ask what they mean. If you are unfamiliar with the area you teach, ask the students what advantages and unique challenges they face living there. Names, language and location are all gateways into your students' cultures. If they can see that you are trying to understand where they come from, they will be more likely to want to understand and engage with you.*

2. Be mindful of things that happen outside the classroom that can affect the 'vibe' inside it. Times of the day, days of the week, weather patterns, holidays and prominent world events can affect how your students feel and will bring that energy into the room. You must learn to read their energy and respond appropriately, channelling it into their learning. Stand at the door before your students come in and observe what they are saying and their body language. For example, if the students are feeling a little hyper because it's a Friday afternoon and 25 degrees outside, perhaps it might be better for them to do a light activity rather than a full-blown revision session. Maintain a little flexibility.**

3. You have to win the hearts and minds of the Disruptors. There are very few ways around it. Unless you can get them permanently removed from your class (which could potentially

create a bigger set of problems down the road), try to get to know them and find out what makes them 'tick'. Talk to other teachers/support staff who seem to have good relationships with them and try to get some tips and strategies to engage them. Give Disruptors responsibilities and tasks to do in your classroom – that shows that you are willing to trust them and give them positive attention, which could be part of why they were being disruptive in the first place! Some Disruptors just want to feel special – give them their chance to shine in a way that helps the classroom rather than destroys it.***

* If you are uncertain about how to deal with students who are from a different context to you, read the chapter "Respect The Culture" in AHT1.

** Reading 'energy' effectively is a critical skill that works in almost every social situation. For more information on how to do this in your classrooms, check out the chapter "Read The Room" in AHT1.

*** Disruptors can be transformed into your greatest allies if handled sensitively and skilfully. The key is to find out their internal motivation and 'bridge' it to what you teach. Look at the chapter "Cast a Vision" in AHT1 for more information.

ARGUE LIKE A PRO: HOW TO HAVE MEANINGFUL CONVERSATIONS IN THE AGE OF SOCIAL MEDIA WITHOUT KICKING OFF

I'm a child of the '80s/'90s. Despite government regulation, I am convinced that children had no rights at the time. When you questioned an adult's instruction, you were hit by four words that shut that convo down. Here they were:

"Because I said so."

That's it. Those words were always the same. Whether grabbing a textbook from the shelf or being asked to parachute out of a plane for a secret mission in Nicaragua.

That wouldn't work for our 21st-Century students now.

Instead, you may get a smirk and a side-eye of defiance if your students are slightly irritated. But if you tick them off, you may find yourself on the receiving end of insults and swear words that would make Eminem proud.

Don't get me wrong, children are not going to be perfect all the time – our twiddlewinks and teenagers will get a bit mouthy – but nowadays, it feels a little different, doesn't it? Have you found yourself sounding like your grandparents, saying, "Kids are out of control nowadays, I'll tell ya!", waving your imaginary walking stick at your class? Do you feel like you can't even have meaningful debates without them turning into arguments about which celebrities belong to secret societies? I think that technology might have something to do with it. Let me explain further.

The Internet's 'Triple Revolution' and How it Affects Your Classroom

As I mentioned, we live through an unprecedented period in human history. Many commentators see the COVID-19 pandemic as the true birth of the Information Age, as most of the planet's population was forced to function online for months during the lockdowns.

The fact that we could function at all (let alone so well) was due to what Harrison Ranie, Lee Rainie and Barry Wellman called 'The Triple Revolution' in their thought-provoking 2012 book, *Networked: The New Social Operating System*. They argued that three critical technological advances have drastically changed how human beings interact and have shaped what we know as modern life today.

The three critical advances were:

1) Broadband

Our jump from dial-up Internet access to stable, high-speed broadband helped unleash the Internet's potential and transformed our daily lives. Broadband allowed us to perform more data-intensive activities, stay online for extended periods, and work seamlessly from home. This also allowed us to create our own content on relatively inexpensive equipment and kick-started the 'digital economy'.

Fun story: in the early noughties, when AOL was still a thing, there used to be a peer-to-peer file sharing program called Limewire. When I discovered I could download music without paying for it, it blew my innocent mind – *the Future was here!* Typically, it would take one hour to download a three-minute song, which was regularly interrupted by my mum's phone calls with aunties about *EastEnders*. When my family upgraded to broadband and the song-stealing process took three minutes, I almost cried tears of joy – that meant I could buy more chicken and chips after school. Thank you, Internet Triple Revolution.

2) Mobile

With the invention of 'next generation mobile phones' that could carry 3G wireless technology, we could now access near broadband level speeds on our phone, allowing us to shop, work and video-call from the palm of our hands. This drastically melted the lines between the different spheres of our life, such as home, school and work, and made us 'digitally mobile' (pun intended).

3) Social Media

The rise of social media changed how we interact with other human beings on a scale that has never been seen in human history. Social media has allowed us to build vast networks with people we would not have been able to connect with in the past. Real-time technology enables us to transact, meet and form relationships with others who could be thousands of miles away.

This has also changed how we view ourselves, as modern life puts on pressure to maintain a 'digital' presence online and share parts of ourselves that would have been seen as private a few decades ago.

Ranie, Rainie and Wellman wrote, "Our research supports the notion that small, densely-knit groups like families, villages and small organisations have receded in recent generations. A different social order has emerged around social networks that are more diverse and less overlapping than previous groups[3]."

Teachers, although these are fantastic technological advances, this is not all sunshine and rainbows. For many of us, this 'triple revolution' has become the banes of our lives, often giving us a triple headache. Trying to take a mobile phone off a youngster is akin to trying to get Boris Johnson to comb his hair. Good luck with that one, mate.

In 2018, the global management consulting group McKinsey wrote a fascinating report called 'True Gen: Generation Z and the Implications for Companies', which charted the fundamental characteristics of Generation Z. They included[4]:

1. Expressing their individual truth – Gen Z'ers believed strongly in the importance of their individual identities and protecting the rights of others to express their own personal truths. In a survey, 70-80% of Gen Z'ers would stop buying from brands who they believed were misogynistic, racist or homophobic.

2. The belief in community – Gen Z'ers are very inclusive and believe that the connections they make online carry the same weight as those they have in real life due to the leaps in mobile

technology. Also, these online communities make it easier for Gen Z'ers to find others with similar interests to share knowledge fluidly.

3. They are more curious and pragmatic – With the vast knowledge that Gen Z'ers have at their fingertips, they can afford to be more critical, analytical and logical with the information they are being presented. 65% of respondents in their survey said 'they value knowing what is happening around them and being in control'. Which is vastly higher than any of the previous generations.

I know what some of you are thinking: "Karl, that sounds all well and dandy mate, but look, I've got to prepare my Year 8 class for their end-of-term tests. So, I'm not teaching them how to make the next Facebook."

OK, Charlie. I get it – but you need to understand the context of where these kids are coming from. So, let's look at what it means for your classrooms.

1. Generation Z want to be respected for who they are and are less likely than previous generations to want to conform. The days of telling them to "Sit down, shut up and open your textbook NOW" are ending. If they feel that you don't respect them for their identities, they will give you a very rough time in the classroom.

2. Generation Z believes in dialogue and will not be afraid to challenge the status quo. We know kids have always rebelled. That is a story as old as time. But doing it on social media isn't. Your students, with an average smartphone, have tools that marketing departments of multinational companies could not even dream of

25 years ago. As many schools have learnt over the past two years, if the students don't believe they're being heard, they can design memes or videos lampooning their school and instantaneously connect with millions of people online. If these videos go viral, they can be picked up by major news publications and broadcasters – it's insane how fast messages travel in the digital universe. Unfortunately, as many teachers have learnt, you don't want to be a national news story.

3. Generation Z students will challenge you and are less likely to stand down. With the information they literally have at hand, students will, more than ever, cross-examine what they are learning and its usefulness in their personal lives. Students up and down the country are telling teachers that 'what they are learning won't help them', and "Why do I need to know about _____ – if I wanted to know it, I could look on Wikipedia."

This can be difficult to handle. Sometimes, it's not a behavioural issue but a generational one.

How to Talk (and Debate) with Generation Z

Let's get to the nitty-gritty details. If your classroom resembles the House of Commons every day and you can't get a word in sideways, that's a problem. If your students are being outright abusive, aggressive or rude, throw the book at 'em: follow your school's behaviour policy.

But... if your students are trying to express an opinion that you may disagree with, but they're showing indications that they are willing to listen, please try these strategies in this section on-for-size. If you learn how to skilfully debate and coach your students, you may be able to turn potential flashpoint situations into teachable moments. Here's how.

1. Avoid Using Absolutes

Several words and phrases are almost guaranteed to up the ante in a potential flashpoint situation.

"Always"

"Ruined"

"Never"

"Impossible"

"Disaster"

"Hate"

"Perfect"

"Must"

"None"

Come on, be honest – I am sure that when you've had an argument with a loved one, you've used these phrases... How did that go for you? If you are like me, it didn't go too well. But if we look at social media tweets/posts/blogs that contain these phrases (and other things that I can't print here), tend to get the most likes/hearts/retweets and shares.

So what is going on here?

Well, it's due to the way that our brains evolved. Our ancient ancestors had to make life and death choices – there was little room for nuance. Most of their options were binary: Die or live another day. Nothing more, nothing less.

But this evolutionary hangover causes us untold problems. Professor Kevin Duttant writes, "We group, we label, we pigeonhole our way into making irrational suboptimal decisions because our brains grew too big too fast[5]." So although most of us don't have to worry about falling trees, predators and rival tribes trying to skin us alive, our nervous system will light up like the Oxford Street Winter Lights at any hint of confrontation, no matter how innocent.

The solution is two-fold: One, as teachers, where you can, please avoid using this language – add nuance to your dialogues. Especially for Disruptors, the use of absolute language gives them little wriggle room and will make them feel that they are doomed to have this label on them forever. I know it's tempting but avoid these labels because they will destroy any rapport that you could potentially build with them. Instead of saying:

"John you are always late, and I hate how you interrupt my lessons."

You could say:

"John, I've noticed that you have been late a couple of times this week and unfortunately interrupted my lessons. So let's discuss how we can sort it out after the lesson."

Which one lands better?

Two: If you have a learner who uses absolute statements, gently reflect their words back to them, adding nuance. Here are a couple of examples:

Sue: *"I will never use quadratic equations in real life. Maths is a waste of time."*

Teacher: *"I understand quadratic equations are not your favourite topic in Maths, but what about sequencing that you enjoyed last week?"*

Example 2:

Toby: *"Learning English is impossible – I will never be good at it."*

Teacher: *"I know English is hard and it's really annoying when you don't get the hang of a subject straight away – but you did really well on the Lady Macbeth module; let's look at what we can do."*

In all the examples above, you have:

a) Acknowledged their feelings.

b) Grown the conversation, which gives you more avenues to explore.

2. Have 'Anti-Social Media Conversations'

Social media is beautiful, but unfortunately, it preys on a mental quirk called confirmation bias. Simply put, "Confirmation bias is the tendency of people to favour information that confirms their existing beliefs or hypotheses. Confirmation bias happens when a person gives more weight to evidence that confirms their beliefs and undervalues evidence that could disprove it[6]."

For example, I believe that Arsenal is the most incredible team in the Premiership. *We are, by the way – any Tottenham supporters, put my book down now.* I will surf the Internet looking up any information that supports my belief, despite the glaring fact that Arsenal, at this time of writing, hasn't won a Premier League title in 20 years, nor have we won a Champions League trophy. But I will filter out any counterclaims from other teams (especially Tottenham).

Sadly, social media companies know this and, using their clever algorithms, will track what I am looking at and offer me more content that supports my beliefs. If I am unaware that this is happening, eventually, all the content I consume will be pro-Arsenal, and I will end up in an echo chamber. The more extreme voices get more engagement and are pushed higher on these platforms. This causes the reasoned debates to become warped and toxic. Although football is mostly harmless, as we have seen in recent years on more serious matters, this can be disastrous and even deadly if unchecked.

How do these behaviours manifest in your classrooms? You may find that your students will be more argumentative and confrontational around the hot topics of the day. This can affect even the meekest learners who, if prompted, will shout and growl like a certain green rage monster in *The Avengers*. But again, throwing your kids out of the classroom may not be the best way to handle it.

Educators, we must learn to listen. I mean it.

This is really important, especially around sensitive topics. We have to first listen to understand, not shoot back. Unless what they say is derogatory, insulting or dangerous, try to get to the core of what the young person is telling you. Simply being sincere in listening to the young person may help calm them down and make the dialogue more civil. Sometimes as teachers, we are too quick to shut down conversations. If they are particularly heated, assure them that you are listening but put in reasonable boundaries like talking to each other calmly, allotting a time limit etc.

3. Play Devil's Advocate

Don't be afraid to make your students aware of confirmation bias and openly (but politely) challenge them to confirm their assumptions. If it's civil enough, ask other students their opinions and see if their view is supported by the majority of the class. Regardless of what subject you teach, we must coach our young people on how they can evaluate the information presented on the Internet. Here are a few questions that I have asked my young people, which may help you guide the conversation.

"How easy would it be for other people to change the information we see?" (Use Wikipedia as an example)

"How do we know that a source is valid?"

"Can we tell the difference between an opinion and fact?"

"Because many people say something is true, does that necessarily mean it is?"

"I can see why you have that viewpoint, but if I presented some new information, would it change your mind?"

This is where I think teaching is absolutely imperative. This is not about changing the young person's mind to support our worldview. On the contrary, this teaches them how to analyse, evaluate and critique information, which is absolutely necessary for the Information Age.

4. Create an Environment Where it is OK to be Wrong

Social media has made it easy to view human interactions as a zero-sum game. There are winners, and there are losers. Us versus Them. The Good Guys versus the Bad Guys. Unfortunately, for the reasons I explained above, this suits our primitive brains to a tee. But in our data-rich world, things are way more complex than that.

Make it clear that this is not about 'winning' and 'losing' – but about sharing ideas. If you make it a 'death battle', of course, this will increase the tension in the group. Instead, you must teach your students that it's OK to have a discussion and 'agree to disagree'. Don't set out to humiliate your students but to educate them. If your student brings up a valid point politely which causes you to change your opinion, then verbally acknowledge their input and gracefully concede to them. Likewise, if you have 'won' the discussion, don't rub it in their face – make it a teachable moment. This is what true education is about – not just pumping our students with facts and figures but giving them the tools to enhance their minds.

Aristotle would be proud.

REFLECTION QUESTIONS

1. When the contentious issues of the day come up in your classroom (i.e. Brexit, racism, homophobia, etc.), do you feel comfortable talking about them? Do you feel nervous that you may get some things wrong? Do you feel equipped to talk about them in a measured way?

2. Post-lockdown, have you noticed an increase in discussions around what is happening on our planet? When your students discuss these topics, how are they communicating their message? Are they nervous/irritable/excited? Does it come from the same individuals, or does it differ depending on the topic?

3. Think about a class that you had taught before where a heated issue was raised. If you can't, think about a time when a contentious issue was brought up in a personal setting. How was this handled? Did it spiral out of control, or did you have a measured discussion? What were the key factors that determined how the debate was conducted?

PRACTICAL TIPS

1. Get informed – As I have highlighted, you will increasingly notice how these hot topics creep into your classroom discussions because of the hyperfast nature of modern media and 24/7 news reporting. Putting our heads in the sand and pretending that these issues 'don't belong in the classroom' will no longer cut it. If an issue keeps cropping up in your classroom and you are uncomfortable discussing it, try finding resources online to help you understand it better. In May 2020, after the tragic murder of George Floyd, many institutions found themselves face to face with the issue of institutional racism, which was reflected in the massive growth of the 'Black Lives Matter' movement. This could no longer be swept under the carpet. The education system led the charge to discuss and unpick this harrowing topic. Out of this dire situation, the tiny silver lining was that many people started to do their research and educate themselves on how to be anti-racist and proactive in creating a fairer society. If your students see that you are trying to get educated on what they care about, they will be more interested in what you care about.*

2. Find the time – Of course, there are caveats. I am not expecting you have a debate every single lesson. And I'm also very aware that some subjects like Citizenship, Geography and English lend themselves better to have these conversations. Nonetheless, you can find creative and innovative ways to encourage these discussions. For example, I have seen Science departments do lessons themed around Alan Turing's work and how his life was

impacted by being a member of the LGBT+ community. Speak to your Head of Department or Curriculum Lead for more advice.

3. It's OK to park discussions – Of course, we have a National Curriculum to teach. It's OK to say to your students what you will NOT discuss. If the subject is particularly contentious or the conversation goes wrong, stop it and tell your students you will revisit it again. If the student is being rude or discriminatory, give them the necessary warnings, and if it continues, enact your behaviour policy. Intolerance and discrimination are never OK, and you must respond robustly to students who cross that line. Sanction as appropriate and, if necessary, pass on your concerns and observations to the pastoral teams.

* If you want more information on how to have sensitive conversations, check out the "Respect The Culture" chapter in AHT1.

HELP THEM MAKE BETTER DECISIONS

It's confession time guys! First, I will list some decisions I made as a teenager that I absolutely cringe at now. Then, I want you to think of your own teenage bone-headed choices and compare them to mine. You ready?

- At 14-years-old, I dyed my hair completely blond to look like the RnB singer Sisqó (remember *Thong Song*?). But my hair looked more like one of the kitchen sponges you buy at the 99p shop.
- At 15, wearing Avirex biker jackets in 30-degree weather to impress the ladies. (I was baking most days, and the smell must have been horrendous.)
- Trying to be a 'gangsta' rapper called Karl Pacino at 16. (I realised very quickly that it sounded too much like the heated beverage 'cappuccino' – an Italian-style coffee doesn't scare anyone.)
- When I was 16, nicking my mate's older brother's birth certificate to try to get into an 'Over 21s' club. (It never ever worked – I don't know why I bothered. I had to do the 'walk of shame' home in front of my so-called friends while they laughed at me.)
- At 17, I took Media Studies as an A-Level when I didn't know what the subject was about.
- At 18, I took a Media Studies/Film-making degree when I DID know what the subject was about and did not study at all.

- At 20 years of age (when I was very intoxicated), I tried to dance like RnB singer Usher to impress a friendly young lady. This was in the middle of Leicester Square in Central London: I managed to trip over my feet and was suddenly teleported to the street below. Her laughter was like a cold blade slicing my soul.

And I could go on and on.

How was your list? I can read your mind, stop lying – I can hear those skeletons jangling in your closet...

Although my life sounds like an episode of *The Inbetweeners*, I prefer to look at those experiences as 'character-building'. Of course, it's easier to do that than cry myself to sleep at night – but this is what we expect from teenagers and young people, don't we?

Now we are 'prim-and-proper' adults, we tend to frown at the behaviour of our more 'rowdy' children. We get outraged when we see Johnny Tableflipper trying to drop kick 11T's 'Little Eugene' like prime Hulk Hogan in *WrestleMania VI*. When we see Meagan Rubberthrower doing the latest TikTok dance in the middle of our classroom, it's easy to look at her and think she's a monster released from some secret military facility.

But we were once them. Our job is to raise our students out of this 'gremlin' phase and make them the lovely, responsible citizens they can be. But first, we need to understand these teens from a social and evolutionary perspective.

Why Do Young People Act Like Idiots Sometimes?

The brain is the most intricate organ in the human body and 'probably the most complex thing in the known universe[7]', according to Professor Sir Robin Murray, one of the UK's leading psychiatrists.

Our brains are made up of little 'command-centres' that are in charge of different aspects of keeping us alive and safe. The two command centres that we are interested in are the amygdala and the prefrontal cortex. The amygdala, located near the centre of the brain, is believed to be in charge of our emotional processes and is linked with memory.

From an evolutionary perspective, researchers believe the amygdala helps us to access threats and pleasures and tie them to our memories for future use. So, the more pleasurable or scary an experience is, the more likely it will stay in your memory. That's why you can remember your favourite holiday in Mexico but not what you had for dinner three weeks ago.

The prefrontal cortex, located just behind our foreheads, is in charge of what is known as our 'executive functions' – which require us to manage ourselves and our environment. Things like planning, decision-making, setting goals and self-control are thought to be housed in this part of our brain.

Here's where it gets interesting: you would think the brain would mature in one whole package right? Not so fast, mon ami... While the amygdala is more or less online straight out of the box, the prefrontal cortex typically matures in your mid to late twenties.

This explains why you, like me, may look at past pictures of yourself and exclaim, "What the heck was I thinking?"

Technically you were, but not with the right part of your brain. Let me explain.

Cold vs Hot Decisions

When one of their students does something worthy of *Candid Camera*, most teachers believe their young people 'don't realise the cost of their actions'. But neuroscience has a slightly different view... Some neuroscientists would say that these teens are fully aware of their decisions but they are unable to process them properly, especially when emotions are involved.

In a broad sense, we as humans make two types of decisions. Cold decisions refer to situations that have low emotional arousal. When we have time and space to think through our options and the stakes are low, we can decide calmly and sequentially. For example, shopping for a winter coat is hardly *The Fast and The Furious*, is it?

Hot decisions are when emotional arousal is high. Significant external pressures such as time constraints, physical and emotional risks or perceived loss may impact your decision-making. For example, if you are a first-aider at the scene of an accident, you will have to make decisions that could mean life or death for the victim. This would be a tense situation.

Under lab conditions, scientists have conducted experiments simulating hot decisions on children and mature adults to see how they respond using brain-imaging technology. These studies revealed that even in tense situations, grown adults process their choices through the prefrontal cortex. In contrast, young people tended to process these high-pressure situations through their amygdala. In a piece written for *The Conversation*, titled "A Parent's Guide To Why Teens Make Bad Decisions", Dr James McCue refers to the link between brain development and poor choices as 'psychosocial maturity[8]'. Further, he states that young people between the ages of 12-23 are more likely to:

- seek excitement and engage in risk-taking behaviour
- make choices on impulse
- focus on short-term gains
- have difficulty delaying gratification
- be susceptible to peer pressure
- fail to anticipate the consequences of their choices.

But before we go further, let's get a little context here...

Are Young People Just Awful?

It might seem like these guys are demons (remember, you used to be like this too), but from an evolutionary perspective, why do teens behave like this? Researchers believe this risky, irritating behaviour may hold an evolutionary advantage by "encouraging separation from the comfort and safety of the natal family, which decreases the chances of inbreeding. The behaviour changes also foster the development and acquisition of independent survival skills[9]." Psychologists would call this process 'differentiation', where the young person pushes away from their caregivers to establish their own identity and will cling more to peers who are going through a similar confusing process.

There's no cure for moody teenagers, I'm afraid. It's all there in our DNA.

With this thought in mind, our job is to help guide and scaffold our young people so they can be themselves without making dumb choices that will destroy their future. Here are a couple of tips:

1. And Then What?

One of the most annoying phrases that I hear from disruptive students when I speak to them about their out-of-control behaviour is:

"Don't worry. Nothing's gonna happen to me."

The arrogance of youth never ceases to amaze me. It doesn't matter if these kids will be excluded or taken in a police car for a crime they have been caught red-handed for – they believe they are superhuman.

As we have discussed, the young person's prefrontal cortex is not developed to understand the gravity of their situation, so we have to help them walk through the possible risks ourselves. My favourite technique to use is what I call "And Then What?" In a calm, measured way, when they tell you the risky action they want to do, your next question should be, "And Then What?" Through the dialogue, sprinkle these responses in and drive the conversation to the hazard that the young person is failing to spot. I will give you a recent example of a conversation I had with a Year 9 student.

K: *"I'm going to punch up that guy that swore at my friend."*

Me: *"And then what?"*

K: *"I'm going to feel better."*

Me: *"But surely you will get caught by the teachers. What will happen after?"*

K: *"I'm going to have to see the Head."*

Me: *"And then what?"*

K: *"I might get permanently excluded."*

Me: *"And then what?"*

K: *"I dunno. I can go to another school, innit?"*

Me: *"But what will happen if you don't get into another school?"*

K: *"It won't be good and I will fail my GCSEs."*

Me: *"And then what?"*

K: *"It will be hard to get a job and I'll have to rely on my mum for money."*

You get the idea. Our young people lack the life experience and thus the foresight to see further ahead. The key to this technique is to let them come out with the responses. Lecturing doesn't work as well because our students often feel they are being dictated to, rather than having the autonomy to make their own decisions. Your job is merely to drive the conversation to where you want it to be – otherwise, they will raise their defences and you will lose the rapport.

2. Help Them to Empathise with Others

In tense situations, we can become 'emotionally hijacked'. When stressed or angry, our empathy can drop, making us more reckless.

If you deal with a student who tends to make decisions to their detriment, try to remind them of how their choices impact the people they love and care about. Or try to get them to understand how the other person may feel by asking them to imagine what it would be like if the shoe was on the other foot. Especially with SEMH students, I have found this a very effective technique to get them to reconsider their actions. I would ask them simple questions like the following:

"What would your mum/brother/carer make of this situation?"

"If someone did that to you, how would you feel?"

"For someone to shout at you, they must have been furious – can you relate?"

These queries get them out of their dysregulated state using their prefrontal cortex. This will make it easier for them to think empathetically and make them less likely to do things that they will regret later.

3. Teach Them How to do a 'Risk Analysis'

Look, you don't have to turn your students into investment bankers – the most essential aspect of this strategy is to get your students 'to think on paper'. With my NEET students, one of the things that I made them do was journal their experiences at the end of the school day. Many scientific research studies have shown that writing about 'difficulties, problems and troubling emotions' forces us to organise our experiences into a sequence, giving us a chance to examine cause and effect and form a coherent story. Through this process, we can also gain some distance from our experiences and begin to understand them in new ways, stumbling upon insights about ourselves and the world[10].

The act of writing calms our nervous system down and can place us in a meditative state. Your students do not have to write *War and Peace* either. A simple pros and cons table or a quick five-minute SWOT analysis could help your student see things on paper that wasn't apparent in their mind. I've done this with primary school children, and it works just as well! Obviously, adjust the exercise to their level of understanding.

4. Teach Them to Own Their 'Next Moves'

One of the complaints about modern education is that we don't teach kids to 'take the initiative' or 'think for themselves'. A relative at a family barbecue once told me that 'teachers were the nation's babysitters'. Charming, I know. But there is a sliver of truth underneath those critiques. When a young person makes a poor decision, it is easy to lecture, to 'fix' the problem and send the child on their merry way. But what we do is rob that young person of the chance to take ownership of the issue and genuinely embed what they have learnt. Then they lack the critical-thinking skills to be able to handle the complexities of the real world.

I learnt this next trick from a brilliant book called *The One Minute Manager Meets the Monkey*, by Ken Blanchard and Hal Burrows. Although this was written in a business context, this can easily apply to education.

In the book, a problem or difficulty is described as a 'monkey'. The next step to solving the problem is called 'the next move'. In management, what tends to happen is subordinates will present their bosses with their 'monkeys' and leave the stressed leader to decide all the next steps. Using the monkey metaphor, the poor manager's office resembles the Ape Section of Chessington Zoo; they're utterly swamped and ineffective. Blanchard and Burrows advised managers not to 'think' for their employees but teach them how to take care of their 'monkeys' themselves. They wrote, "As a manager, to the extent that you can get people to care for and feed their own monkeys, they are really managing the work themselves[11]."

What does that look like in a classroom? Let me help you by giving you an example.

Imagine Johnny Tableflipper had a fight in your classroom, and now he's with you in after-school detention. There's a pending investigation, and the detention's outcome will be factored into his final sanction. The 'monkey' in this situation is how to resolve the incident. The typical way of resolving these problems would be to get Johnny to do his detention, scold him for his bad behaviour, tell him to apologise to the other kid and dust off your hands. But what has Johnny really learnt? You have taken the onus off him and added it to your ever-increasing workload. Here's what you should do:

A) Ask Johnny to identify three possible resolutions. For example, Johnny chose three options: a phone call home, an inclusion day, or being let off the hook.

B) Get Johnny to explain his reasoning on why he chose those decisions. You can then help him walk through the positives and negatives of each situation.

C) Ask Johnny to think like a teacher: ask him what he would do if you were his student. This will require him to empathise and reflect on his own behaviour.

D) You make a final decision based on what you are both happy with.

Although it might take slightly longer to do than just giving Johnny the 'hairdryer treatment', this is helping Johnny improve his decision-making and deeply embed that his actions have consequences. This will also take the mental strain off your beautiful head, which is always a good thing.

Lastly, it makes Johnny feel he has self-determination on what happens to him and is more likely to comply with the decision as he helped devise it. Although I have used it for a sanction, this can be used for almost anything. And don't stop with just the kids you teach. If you have leadership responsibilities, use this technique with your staff – this helps make delegation a breeze.

REFLECTION QUESTIONS

1. Do you have the same students repeatedly making bad decisions? How have you dealt with it in the past? Emotionally, how do you feel when they keep on repeating these behaviours?

2. When your students repeat these negative patterns, do they make promises to change? If they do, how sincere are they with their efforts? What do you think holds them back?

3. Do you regularly delegate tasks to your students/colleagues? If you don't, then what is holding you back? When you have delegated things in the past, how well did it go?

PRACTICAL TIPS

1. As a classroom teacher, I realise you may not have time to use all the techniques in this chapter – some of you have hundreds of kids to teach in the academic year! But these techniques really shine when you are talking to Compliants and Disruptors on a one-to-one level. If you build relationships with these disruptive students, you will find that these tools will help you coach them to make the right decisions. If you facilitate a detention with a student, rather than sitting in silence, try a couple of these techniques during this detention time or restorative meeting. It can help you build up that rapport that may help prevent it in the future*.

2. How you approach the situation is just as important as what you say in these interactions. I know some of these students can be incredibly annoying, but try to keep your tone as relaxed and playful as possible. Especially after a serious incident, remember that these students can be 'emotionally hijacked' and are less likely to hear what you have to say. Speak slowly and listen intently – if you learn to pick out the right things in the conversation, you will find you get to the bottom of the issues faster and easier.

3. Initially, getting into this 'coaching' mode may be challenging if the student has a hostile relationship with you. This is where you will need to call for backup. Get your pastoral team involved, ask other teachers who have a positive relationship with that student if they have any strategies to deal with them, and ask if they could possibly join you if you conduct a restorative meeting. Shameless

plug here – in AHT1, there is a whole section dedicated to building up rapport with complex learners, called 'The Good' – use any of the techniques in there and once you get a little 'buy-in' from your student, then come back to this chapter.

* If you need help on how to communicate with an emotionally-hijacked student, check out the "Use Last" chapter in AHT1. It's a brilliant framework used by telephone account managers that I adapted for the classroom. Have a look!

BE A GIVER: HOW TO USE 'THE LAW OF RECIPROCITY' TO ENHANCE YOUR CLASSROOM RELATIONSHIPS

Have you ever been given an unexpected gift by someone and you felt the overwhelming need to return the favour?

Or have you ever done a favour for someone and forgot about it, only for that person to surprise you with help and remind you how you helped them?

Then my friend, you have seen the 'law of reciprocity' at work.

The law of reciprocity is a very prevalent social norm in human society. Simply put, it means that 'if someone does something nice for you, you have the built-in tendency to want to do something nice for them[12]'. This social norm exists in every human relationship; from business to romantic relationships, giving and receiving are integral to the human experience.

Although other animal groups have shown they can share, they do not do it on the scale of human beings. Despite the evidence of how incredibly selfish and destructive human beings can be, there is a side of us that still shows love, kindness and empathy. Even Charles Darwin, the brilliant evolutionary scientist who developed the 'Natural Selection Theory' and coined the term 'survival of the fittest' was baffled at human altruism. Cultural anthropologists like Richard Leakey believe that our early human ancestors "would not have survived unless they did something that no animals of other species have been known to do (which was) to regularly share their food with each other[13]."

Our altruism caused us to form communities, which led to us as a species to create civilisation – and led us to build our complex society of iPhones and Amazon packages that we enjoy today.

So, let me take off my nerd glasses for a second and jump back into the classroom – why is this important to you, the stressed teacher dealing with the students who want to break your mind and your spirit? It's simple: This drive within us can be activated and used to create rapport and goodwill and make us do things we may not have wanted to do. In fact, many marketing departments of the world's biggest brands rely on this drive within us to sell their products. Here are some examples:

- Getting taster samples in the supermarket to entice you to buy a new chocolate bar.
- The one-month free trial of the popular software you really want.
- Free resources, eBooks and content delivered to your email if you sign unto a new website (I've used this one).
- Special discounts and gifts at random times from your favourite store.
- Special benefits and perks to recognise employee contributions to the company.

And so on. It's all around us. Before discussing how this works in your classrooms, I want to address the 'elephant-in-the-room'.

This can feel a little... icky. And trust me, despite having to sell and brand my own products, I still struggle with this. Modern business practices and stories of huge companies using PR machines to cover up their bad behaviour have made us understandably sceptical of how these social principles can trick other people.

The techniques I will discuss can be used to manipulate others, but that is not what it is about. Therefore, we will not use the 'Dark Side of the Force'.

Forgive me if I sound like a Zen master, but it's all about intention. These techniques should be used:

A) To help build positive relationships with your students.

B) To help your students be the best versions of themselves possible.

C) For the betterment of everyone in your classroom to make it a harmonious, inclusive environment.

Our young people have powerfully-attuned BS monitors – if your intentions are not pure, they will not hesitate to call you out on it. I presume you became a teacher because you believed you could change lives and create a better tomorrow for your students. If you give from the heart, you will never become a teaching Sith lord, I promise you.

OK, now that we have that out of the way, let's talk about ways to give to our students that will hit our three Jedi objectives.

1. Show Appreciation

It might seem obvious, but after training teachers for almost four years, many educators still struggle to do this. You may have been told not to "smile at your students until December". Please throw that advice in the bin. Verbally show appreciation. If someone does something thoughtful to you or others in your classroom, say it. If your student has been struggling with the work and they have overcome that challenge, say it. If you have a kid who you know has difficulties at home and managed to get to your classroom on time, say it. It's all these little things that can make a world of difference. Trust me, I was one of those kids, and small acts of kindness could make or break my day. Please be conscientious.

2. Give Something Meaningful

This could be to an individual or to the entire classroom. Obviously, please don't spend a million pounds! Ensure it is within professional and ethical boundaries and doesn't violate your Code of Practice. If you are within these boundaries and your students have done something great, don't just give them the usual movie and pizza sessions; try to give them something that they will remember and will resonate with them long after they leave your classroom.

A great colleague of mine looks after a group of students that have severe SEN needs. Because of their learning difficulties, they are often academically at the bottom of their classes. To make them feel special, at the end of every academic year, he organises a 'TED Talk' to which the whole school is invited. These kids talk about any subject of their choosing for 10 minutes and are encouraged to bring props and wear costumes. There are various prizes for the students, who get to take pictures with their favourite teachers and peers. I'm always in awe of how a couple of hours at the end of the year can brighten up these students' school experience. You don't have to do what my colleague does but don't underestimate the power of creating experiences for your students to enjoy.

3. Incentivise Your Students (the Right Way)

Yes, do your star charts, merits or whatever reward systems you have in place, but please base your praises on effort rather than results. This is critical for students who have SEN or SEMH difficulties, as they may feel they can never catch up to their mainstream peers. Results-based praise may make them more demotivated if they compare themselves to their peers. In the same way you differentiate between their academic lessons, differentiate for your reward systems.

4. Give Small and Often

Please do not do an 'Oprah'. In 2004, Oprah infamously gave away hundreds of brand-new cars to her studio audience who couldn't afford a vehicle. Although the gesture was terrific, it ultimately backfired because it cost each new car owner up to $7,000 to register the 'gift'. Although it is extreme, this is a great example of 'negative reciprocity'. If we are given inappropriate gifts, they have the opposite effect, making the receiver feel suspicious, indebted and even resentful. They may feel you are trying to 'buy' their favour and use this as a bargaining tool later. Keep it small - preferably to cheap gifts, resources, activities, and keep it professional. Giving the wrong thing could land you in hot water – use the 'Line Manager Test' as guidance.

REFLECTION QUESTIONS

1. If students do well in your classrooms, how do you reward them? Do you follow the school's policy, or do you have one of your own? How do you determine who gets rewarded?

2. How often do you show appreciation to your students? If you don't, what is stopping you? If you do, then how do your students respond to your praise?

3. Have you ever tried to create an 'experience' for your students? If you did, how did it go? If you haven't, what constraints are stopping you and could they be removed?

PRACTICAL TIPS

1. If you deal with SEMH students, this is probably the most essential tip in this book. For the reasons I have discussed in previous chapters, many of them could have environmental factors that hindered them from developing the stable relationships needed to thrive. As a result, they may display hostile behaviours – not because of you personally but because they have not learned to trust anyone in any relationship. This is what can make educating them incredibly challenging. In my 12 years of teaching, showing appreciation has been one of the cornerstones of dealing with SEMH children, as sometimes I knew I was the only adult in their life who did this regularly. Please practice this, especially in these difficult times that we are all facing.

2. Do not be scared to give your students choices. As I have mentioned in previous chapters, especially for teenagers, giving them autonomy and responsibility is a way to make them feel special and shows that you trust them too. If the class have done exceptionally well, give them options on how a future lesson can be facilitated and take in their ideas – they may surprise you.

3. Creating classroom experiences doesn't need a Marvel movie's production values – it can be surprisingly cheap. For one of my challenging SEMH classes at the end of the academic year, I organised a 'Games Day' where I bought a pack of cards, Monopoly board, ginger beers and popcorn, and played some banging tracks courtesy of YouTube. We had a great time discussing what happened over the last 12 months and the whole experience only cost me 20 quid. Be creative – beg, borrow and steal from other departments and make a day they won't forget. It will do absolute wonders for your classroom relationships going forward.

EPILOGUE

EPILOGUE

THANK YOU MS PEARCE

There we have it. Thank you for rocking with me to the end of *The Action Hero Teacher 2* – I will always appreciate it.

Hopefully, this book has equipped you with the tools, tips and strategies to teach, engage and lead even the most challenging Generation Z (and Alpha) learners you will face in your career.

But with this book, I want to end with something different.

I want to end with a story. My story.

You see, I wasn't always this dashing, articulate specimen of a man that you see before your eyes – when I was little, I had a troubled childhood and really hated school.

For reasons I won't go into, I was a very angry, unhappy, rebellious little boy that always picked fights, never listened to anybody and generally wanted to cause havoc.

My motto would have been, 'If life is s%$ for me, why don't I make it bad for everyone else?'

Then Ms Pearce came into my life.

When I joined her Year 6 class, I was really off the rails. I gained a bit of a reputation, which I revelled in and at the same time secretly despised. But when she was teaching me, she looked at me differently than the other teachers. Through her mahogany eyes, she saw the real me. Not the brash, rude, wild child but the boy who was hurting, misunderstood and needed someone to believe in him.

Ms Pearce always smiled at me and, most of the time, listened to me patiently and kindly. She gave me responsibilities and care, while other teachers told her she was foolish to nurture me. Yet, she always trusted and believed I would eventually make the right decisions.

She made me 6B's book monitor, and although my career was patchy at best, this is what helped my love of reading to flourish. In 'show-and-tell', when the other students groaned when I brought yet another book to review, she beamed and encouraged me to speak on the things I cared about.

But I wasn't always nice to Ms Pearce. Sometimes I would shout at her, be rude, throw things, and hit out because I was 'emotionally hijacked'. Looking back on it now, I know I must have been tough to deal with. There must have been times when she wanted to give up on me. Times where she might have wanted me to be removed from her group.

But she didn't. She sanctioned me appropriately but always told me that she knew that I would come good. She believed in me when I didn't believe in it myself.

Several decades later, here I am. I wish I could tell you that everything fell into place when I left primary school – it didn't. It took a looooooong time for the seeds Ms Pearce planted in me to truly blossom. But they eventually did.

EPILOGUE

I genuinely believe that the first turning point in my life was when I was taught by Ms Pearce. I recently tried to find her to thank her for being such a wonderful teacher. But alas, I was unsuccessful. Even with the mighty Internet, I don't know what became of her. But I sincerely hope that somehow, she gets to read this chapter and know how much she means to me. Part of the reason I can do what I do is that she took a chance on me when no one else bothered to do so.

Thank you, Ms Pearce.

Dear educators, in your career, you may educate hundreds, possibly thousands of students in your tenure. Yet, as time goes on, you may forget their names and faces as they descend into the sea of your memory.

But if you are the outstanding teachers I imagine you to be, they will never forget you. This gig can be incredibly hard, and there will be times that you just want to chuck in the towel. But remember, you are planting seeds in your students that can change their lives for the better – and they will be forever indebted to you. As a teacher:

You can make a difference.
You will make a difference.
And you must make a difference.

The world needs educators like you more than ever before. Despite all the mayhem that seems to be blighting this world, your classroom may be the only sanctuary of peace your students have.

You can be the teacher that helps your Generation Z (and Alpha) students bounce back. You can turn around your lost class.

I wish you all the best in your teaching career. Thank you for reading.

See you around.

Karl C. Pupé FRSA

CONTACT PAGE

Website: www.actionheroteacher.com

Email: contact@actionheroteacher.com

Twitter: @actionheroteach

Instagram: @actionheroteacher

TikTok: @actionheroteacher

Don't hesitate to reach out!

ACKNOWLEDGEMENTS

Thank you GOD for another opportunity to share my work in the world. Thank you for everything you do for me.

To Natalie and Isabella – You are my motivation to keep pushing through and to continue pressing on. Thank you for your patience, understanding and love.

To Uncle Eric Odotei – You are the Cristiano Ronaldo of advice and strategy. You always come in clutch. Thank you for your timely wisdom, guidance & encouragement. You know how much I appreciate you.

To Viv Groskop – Thank you so much for championing my work and writing the foreword. Thank you for inviting me on your podcast when I was starting out. It is still one of the highlights of my career!

To all my former students – (You know who you are). You made teaching worth it. Thank you for being my teaching me to stay curious, humble and not take life so seriously. You guys are the future – it ain't just a song.

Lastly, thank you readers – Some of you have rocked with me since the start of the AHT journey. You have shared my blogs, recommended people to follow me, and sent me words of encouragement. You will never realise how vital those positive interactions were – especially in the not-so-good times. I am here because of your support. Thank you.

BIBLIOGRAPHY

SECTION 1 Introduction

1. Carrey, J., 2021. Before You Diagnose Yourself With Depression. [online] iFunny.com. Available at: https://ifunny.co/picture/jim-carrey-before-you-diagnose-yourself-with-depression-or-low-sbaT5oWr8.

SECTION 2 Teaching Generation Z

1. The Online Cambridge Dictionary. 2021. Definition of 'generation'. [ONLINE] Available at: https://dictionary.cambridge.org/dictionary/english/generation.

2. James, W., 2013. The Principles of Psychology Volume 1. New York: Cosimo, p.121.

3. Fast Company. 2015. What It Takes To Change Your Brain's Patterns After Age 25. [ONLINE] Available at: https://www.fastcompany.com/3045424/what-it-takes-to-change-your-brains-patterns-after-age-25.

4. Greene, R., 2018. The Laws of Human Nature. 1st ed. London, UK: Profile Books. Page 539.

5. Strauss, W., 1997. Fourth Turning: What the Cycles of History Tell Us about America's Next Rendezvous with Destiny. Crown Publishing Group (NY), p.3.

6. Dalio, R., 2021. Principles for dealing with the changing world order. Simon and Schuster UK, p.36.

7. KPMG. 2017. Meet the Millennials. [ONLINE] Available at: https://home.kpmg/content/dam/kpmg/uk/pdf/2017/04/Meet-the-Millennials-Secured.pdf.

8. Deloitte. 2019. UK Millennials and Generation Z feel unsettled about the future. [ONLINE] Available at: https://www2.deloitte.com/uk/en/pages/press-releases/articles/millennials-and-generation-z-feel-unsettled-about-the-future.html.

9. YPulse. 2020. This Is How Gen Z and Millennials Have Changed Activism. [ONLINE] Available at: https://www.ypulse.com/article/2020/07/14/this-is-how-gen-z-millennials-have-changed-activism/

10. Opinions of Generation Z's ambitions and priorities differ greatly between the generations. 2017. Ipsos MORI. [ONLINE] Available at: https://www.ipsos.com/ipsos-mori/en-uk/opinions-generation-zs-ambitions-and-priorities-differ-greatly-between-generations

11. McCrindle. 2022. Understanding Generation Alpha - McCrindle. [online] Available at: https://mccrindle.com.au/insights/blog/gen-alpha-defined/

12. Gwi.com. 2022. Generation Alpha: the real picture. [online] Available at: https://www.gwi.com/reports/gen-alpha

13. Trifonova, V., 2022. 4 insights on Gen Alpha: How their online behaviors are changing. GWI. Available at: https://blog.gwi.com/trends/4-insights-on-gen-alpha/

SECTION 3 The Basics

1. Wikipedia, (2002), Maslow's Hierarchy of Needs [ONLINE]. Available at: https://en.wikipedia.org/wiki/Maslow%27s_hierarchy_of_needs#/media/File:MaslowsHierarchyOfNeeds.svg

2. Mason, C., 2022. Nearly half of state school teachers 'plan to quit within five years'. [online] Tes Magazine. Available at: https://www.tes.com/magazine/news/general/nearly-half-state-school-teachers-plan-quit-within-five-years

SECTION 4 Escalation

1. YoungMinds. 2022. Mental Health Statistics UK | Young People. [online] Available at: https://www.youngminds.org.uk/about-us/media-centre/mental-health-statistics/ (change the wording to 'based on surveys and reports taken over a number of years.)

2. SEMH. 2022. SEMH Meaning - What does SEMH mean? - SEMH. [online] Available at: https://semh.co.uk/social-emotional-and-mental-health-semh/semh-meaning-what-is-semh/

3. Department for Education, 2015. Special educational needs and disability code of practice: 0 to 25 years, p.16. https://assets.publishing.service.gov.uk/government/uploads/system/uploads/attachment_data/file/398815/SEND_Code_of_Practice_January_2015.pdf

4. GOV.UK. 2022. When a mental health condition becomes a disability. [online] Available at: https://www.gov.uk/when-mental-health-condition-becomes-disability#:~:text=A%20mental%20health%20condition%20is,likely%20to%20last%2C%2012%20months.

5. Bowlby, J., 2005. Clinical applications of attachment theory. London, New York: Routledge Classics, p.4.

6. Cherry, K., 2022. What You Should Know About Attachment Styles. [online] Verywell Mind. Available at: <https://www.verywellmind.com/attachment-styles-2795344#:~:text=Based%20on%20these%20observations%2C%20Ainsworth,known%20as%20disorganized%2Dinsecure%20attachment>

7. School of Life., 2019. How to Overcome Your Childhood. London: School of Life Press, The, p.16.

8. Up.org.uk. 2022. Social, Emotional and Mental Health – Unlocking Potential. [online] Available at: <https://up.org.uk/social-emotional-mental-health/>

9. Edward, T., 2019. TIMPSON REVIEW OF SCHOOL EXCLUSION. [ebook] Westminister: Department for Education, pp.36, 105. Available at: <http://data.parliament.uk/DepositedPapers/Files/DEP2019-0527/Timpson_Review_of_School_Exclusion_May_2019.pdf>

10. 2016. Understanding the educational background of young offenders - Joint experimental statistical report from the Ministry of Justice and Department for Education. [ebook] Ministry of Justice, Department for Education, p.3. Available at: <https://assets.publishing.service.gov.uk/government/uploads/system/uploads/attachment_data/file/577542/understanding-educational-background-of-young-offenders-full-report.pdf>

11. Encyclopedia Britannica. 2022. habit. [online] Available at: <https://www.britannica.com/topic/habit-behaviour>

12. Kirsch, K., 2021. The Salesperson's Guide to Pattern Interrupt. [online] Blog.hubspot.com. Available at: <https://blog.hubspot.com/sales/pattern-interrupt#:~:text=What%20is%20pattern%20interrupt%3F,into%20another%20state%20of%20mind.>

13. Klotz, M., 2022. Loss Aversion - Everything You Need to Know | InsideBE. [online] InsideBE. Available at: <https://insidebe.com/articles/loss-aversion/>

14. BehavioralEconomics.com | The BE Hub. 2022. Loss aversion. [online] Available at: <https://www.behavioraleconomics.com/resources/mini-encyclopedia-of-be/loss-aversion/>

15. The Decision Lab. 2022. Negativity Bias - The Decision Lab. [online] Available at: <https://thedecisionlab.com/biases/negativity-bias>

16. Tierney, J. and Baumeister, R., 2019. The Power of Bad And How to Overcome It. Great Britain: Penguin Random House UK, p.11.

17. Voss, C. and Raz, T., 2016. Never Split The Difference. London: Penguin Random House UK, p.72.

SECTION 5 Disengagement/Hostility

1. Jung, C. and Jacobi, J., 1986. Psychological reflections. London: Routledge, p.19.

2. Groskop, V., (2018). How to Own the Room: Women and the Art of Brilliant Speaking. Bantam Press, p.33.

3. Covey, S., (2007). The 8th habit, from effectiveness to greatness. 1st ed. Simon and Schuster UK, p.42.

4. Maxwell, J. C. (2006). The 360 [degree symbol] leader : developing your influence from anywhere in the organization. Nashville: Nelson Business, p.100.

5. Cambridge Dictionary (2020). SATIRE | meaning in the Cambridge English Dictionary. [online] Cambridge.org. Available at: https://dictionary.cambridge.org/dictionary/english/satire

6. Čomić, M. (2019). Why satirical news sites matter for society. [online] What's New in Publishing | Digital Publishing News. Available at: https://whatsnewinpublishing.com/why-satirical-news-sites-matter-for-society/.

7. Covey, S. M. R. and Merrill, R. R. (2018). The Speed of Trust : the one thing that changes everything. New York: Free Press, p.2.

8. Miles, T. (2020). ONE 'extraordinary call' convinced Liverpool chief Klopp was right man. [online] Mail Online. Available at: https://www.dailymail.co.uk/sport/football/article-7898937/Liverpool-chief-reveals-ONE-extraordinary-conversation-convinced-Klopp-right-man-Reds.html

9. Sheen, T. (2015). Klopp believes Liverpool will win the title in the next four years. [online] Independent Online. Available at: https://www.independent.co.uk/sport/football/premier-league/jurgen-klopp-believes-liverpool-will-win-the-title-in-the-next-four-years-and-describes-himself-as-the-normal-one-a6687446.html

10. Siregar, C. (2021). What is heavy metal football and how has Jürgen Klopp used it at Liverpool? | Goal.com. [online] Available at: https://www.goal.com/en-gb/news/what-is-heavy-metal-football-how-has-jurgen-klopp-used-it-at/gvxzni0i7rne1enr3bayptwcr

11. Herbert, I. (2017). Liverpool coach reveals Jürgen Klopp's methods and says he is '30% tactics, 70% team building'. The Independent. [online] 16 Jan. Available at: https://www.independent.co.uk/sport/football/premier-league/liverpool-news-jurgen-klopp-coach-reveals-methods-tactics-team-building-epl-a7529936.html

12. Hunter, A. (2020). Trust, patience and hard work: how Jürgen Klopp transformed Liverpool. [online] Available at: https://www.theguardian.com/football/2020/jun/26/trust-patience-and-hard-work-how-jurgen-klopp-transformed-liverpool

13. Dakin, G. (2021). Be more Batman : face your fears and look good doing it. London: Dorling Kindersley Limited, p.46.

14. Greene, R. (2000). The 48 Laws of Power. London: Profile, p.79-80.

SECTION 6 Audience

1. William Von Hippel (2018). The Social Leap : the new evolutionary science of who we are, where we come from, and what makes us happy. New York: Harper Wave, An Imprint Of Harpercollinspublishers, p.20.

2. Greene, R. (2020). The Concise Laws of Human Nature. Profile Books, p.216-217.

3. Rainie, H. Ranie, L and Wellman, B. (2014). Networked : the new social operating system. Cambridge: Mit Press, p8-9.

4. Francis, T. and Hoefel, F. (2018). 'True Gen': Generation Z and its implications for companies. [online] McKinsey and Company. Available at: https://www.mckinsey.com/industries/consumer-packaged-goods/our-insights/true-gen-generation-z-and-its-implications-for-companies.

5. Dr Kevin Dutton (2021). BLACK AND WHITE THINKING : the burden of a binary brain in a complex world. S.L.: Corgi, p.9.

6. Noor, I. (2020). Confirmation Bias | Simply Psychology. [online] www.simplypsychology.org. Available at: https://www.simplypsychology.org/confirmation-bias.html

7. BBC. (2012). The brain is the 'most complex thing in the universe'. (2012). BBC News. [online] 29 May. Available at: https://www.bbc.co.uk/news/uk-scotland-18233409

8. McCue, J. (2018). A parent's guide to why teens make bad decisions. [online] The Conversation. Available at: https://theconversation.com/a-parents-guide-to-why-teens-make-bad-decisions-88246#:~:text=Cold%20situations%20are%20choices%20made

9. Johnson, S. B., Blum, R. W. and Giedd, J. N. (2009). Adolescent Maturity and the Brain: The Promise and Pitfalls of Neuroscience Research in Adolescent Health Policy. Journal of Adolescent Health, [online] 45(3), pp.216–221. doi:10.1016/j.jadohealth.2009.05.016 https://www.ncbi.nlm.nih.gov/pmc/articles/PMC2892678/

10. Newman, K. M. (2020). How Journaling Can Help You in Hard Times. [online] Greater Good. Available at: https://greatergood.berkeley.edu/article/item/how_journaling_can_help_you_in_hard_times

11. Blanchard, K. H., Oncken, W. and Burrows, H. (2011). The One Minute Manager® Meets the monkey : free up your time and deal with priorities. London: Harpercollins Publishers, p.74.

12. Apodaca, M. (2020). How to Use the Law of Reciprocity for Effective Persuasion. [online] Available at: https://www.lifehack.org/871383/law-of-reciprocity

13. Rousseau, M. F. (1991). Community : the tie that binds. Lanham, Md.: University Press of America, p.103.

Printed in Great Britain
by Amazon